WATCHER

JASON STOKES

Gestalt Media

Copyright © 2019 by Jason Stokes

First paperback edition March 2019

Cover Design by: Lindy Martin
ISBN 978-1-7337355-0-6 (paperback)
ISBN 978-1-7337355-1-3 (ebook)

www.Gestalt-Media.com

For Anna, who inspires me every day.

Author's Note

I wrote this novel for my wife who has suffered the devastating effects of Multiple Sclerosis as a diagnosed patient for the last six years with symptoms many years before that. It is with the greatest respect for the MS community and those with similar hurdles to cross every day that I crafted a character who I hope will live up to the reality of lives spent struggling to do what most of us take for granted. For those who sometimes have to accept getting out of bed as a personal victory and understand the frustration of not living up to your own expectations. It was my deepest wish to shine light on not only the difficulties faced with this terrible disease but the spirit and the *abilities* that are still present in the many wonderful people who continue to do battle with themselves every single day. I can only hope that Teri and her boundless determination are a small moment of joy for you and a chance to know that you are not alone.

Ch. 1

Teri ignored the message that flashed on the desktop. Whoever wanted her attention right now would have to wait. In the top drawer of her desk, she kept a handblown glass pipe. It was a souvenir from the Bahamas. Something she'd picked up two—or maybe it had been three—years ago. The last time she'd gone anywhere that might be considered a vacation. They said when you retired, it was like a permanent vacation. They were wrong. Teri was twenty-seven and medically retired, and her life was far removed from days spent lounging in the shade, reading good books and reveling in boundless free time. It was dull, it was monotonous and as fall crept in on the sleepy mountain town where she was born and raised, it was a haze of frigid mornings, tepid afternoons and endless redundant nights.

Hidden away in her nest on the third floor of a renovated building off Patton, Teri lit what remained in the pipe. Just resin now, not enough for a decent buzz. Not even enough to knock the edge off nerves that had wound tighter as the day wore on. Now as rush hour set in, the squeal of brakes and horns began their symphony beyond the single-paned window. Her legs burned, her back ached and the familiar sensation that hot water rushed through her veins had started early. She would take what was available.

Open flame made the resin crackle, then pop, and she coughed bringing it in. She exhaled the thick cloud in a long, slow motion, savoring the end of her supply. That was an ounce, a month's worth. There were still two weeks in September, which meant it was time to cut back. She dropped the pipe in the drawer, slammed it shut. *Fat chance.*

Another shipment would take three days. She could make it that long. It wouldn't be fun, but if she cut the grocery budget, got lucky on a few sales, worked out a trade or two, it could be done. That was a task for later. She wrote it out on a Post-it note to remind herself, stuck it to the monitor and turned to the message, still blinking with mechanical precision on the desktop.

`Baclofen?`, was all it said.

She could handle that. A month's supply or maybe more, depending on how much she could give up. It was early, though. Teri wasn't the only one who needed to cut back. She recognized the screen name as a frequent customer's and typed back what she had on hand.

`100 x 10mg Standard price.`

Standard price was twenty-five bucks, a steal when a month's supply went for four times that at a pharmacy. Baclofen was a generic muscle relaxer. For junkies and pill addicts there was stronger stuff, better stuff. For patients with chronic illness like spinal injuries or multiple sclerosis, it was a cheap-by-insurance-standards prescription that battled a common symptom known as muscular spasticity, an involuntary contraction of the muscles.

With insurance it was easy to get, and most plans covered it. Without it, you had to know someone and even then it could get expensive. No one just needed baclofen. It was a support drug, one ingredient in a pharmaceutical cocktail and since no one should have to choose between having food on the table and a few minutes of relief each day, she sold what she could and then some.

Will take all, thanks, he responded.

They shared only screen names and a shipping alias. It was a good system. The buyer, in this case Mr. Lincoln, ordered the same prescription to a post office box in Phoenix, Arizona, once a month, more or less on schedule. The package arrived in a nondescript plain envelope with a return address of the pharmaceutical company that produced the medication. Teri didn't know what disease Mr. Lincoln treated with his medication, but he was consistent and discreet.

She pasted a payment address into the window and waited. When the confirmation came, she would pack a bottle of the wonder pills and ship them out over the weekend. They would reach Mr. Lincoln by Monday, Tuesday at the latest.

With a click the window closed again.

As she was stuck in limbo between Medicaid and disability, the government still paid for pills that didn't work but refused basic expenses like food and shelter. Selling her prescriptions to those who couldn't afford them or couldn't afford insurance to get a prescription gave Teri a sense of purpose. It felt good to help others suffering through a broken system. Digital currencies kept her shielded from law enforcement agencies, and the income was enough to keep her going until the disability courts decided her fate. Keeping her mind occupied so she didn't go nuts in the meantime was a little more difficult.

She fixed a second Post-it note with a reminder to mail the package on the monitor and turned her attention to a live feed. Five windows spread across the desktop showed rooms from a suburban home on a cul-de-sac somewhere across town.

A ceiling-mounted camera showed an empty living room: Ashley furniture, oversized television and glass-topped coffee table that waited in digitized silence. Another camera overlooked the pool.

In-ground pools were a luxury at this altitude, even one small by most standards. In the summer, Allie, a fortyish brunette and mother of two, spent her afternoons doing laps in the cramped confines. Now that it was too cold for swimming, a tarp stretched across the surface to keep leaves from clogging the drain, and Allie read trashy novels in a metal chair on the patio. She was joined often by a glass of red wine. The covers were too distant to read, but Teri bet they had the words "cowboy" and "stud" on them.

A camera mounted in the front entryway revealed bare hooks where there had been jackets and backpacks. A space underneath for shoes, empty except for a single pair. The family dog, an aging golden retriever, ambled through the frame, tail hung low with a lazy twitch.

Teri sighed.

"Daytime TV sucks."

The feed that monitored Allie's front walk had been flickering for weeks. Now it was black. She toyed with the idea of slinking over in the afternoon when no one was home to repair the connection but thought better of it. Too much risk to watch the neighbor's grass grow. Grass that was greenest where a stray lab mix crapped on it, in the same place, every day.

According to reverse lookup, the off-white, two-story home belonged to Allison and Brandon Shurmer. Allison spent mornings and evenings at home. Where she went during the day was a mystery. She didn't wear gym clothes and rarely returned with shopping bags, but she was away for several hours almost every afternoon.

Brandon was harder to find information on except for a vehicle registration on a two-year-old blue Civic that he preferred to park in the garage, using a side door to the kitchen instead of the front. A kitchen Teri had never seen, because none of the interior cameras pointed that way, but since the developers had built all the homes in this neighborhood from the same blueprint, the Shurmers' kitchen was identical to at least five others on different feeds. Each home was an alternate-dimension version of the others. A bowl of plastic fruit on one counter instead of flowers, silver-finished appliances instead of black, but otherwise the same.

The Civic stayed indoors. A double-wide expanse of oil-stained concrete that passed as a driveway in this neighborhood got its stain from a rusted work truck that parked there on Saturday nights. The dented vanity plate's letters, FUL TLT, had been registered to Ryan Shurmer, Allie's brother-in-law, online poker addict and, Teri suspected, a mooch.

Except for Lisa, the oldest daughter, fifteen, pot smoker and cheerleader, who Teri had seen more than once sneak through the shadows to a car parked down the street at two a.m., there was no good drama in the Shurmer household.

The Shurmers were average, predictable ... boring.

A tap of the Esc key and the windows closed. In their place a black screen with a blinking white cursor waited for commands. Teri entered a new string and hit Enter. The window filled with lines of information. The program was her own design, built on top of code she'd found online and altered to suit her purpose. Right now a bot was searching a list of local IPs scanning for vulnerabilities.

The bot focused on a range of ports associated with webcams, security systems or anything with a live feed. She limited IPs to those from a local service provider, which ensured all returned addresses came from her neighbors and the city that surrounded them.

Teri liked her city and the people that lived in it as much as you could when you rarely spent time outside. She liked that security in this area was low, due to a cultural awareness that leaned away from technology.

Asheville was a city built on diversity. Known for the duality of the überrich who flocked to the region for its gorgeous— and expensive—scenery and the trendy counterculture of downtown drum circles and healing crystals. The characters were eccentric, the stories near endless, and most played out on unsecured networks.

Unsecured to Teri meant that her targets were satisfied with the bare minimum. Typical homeowners trusted their security system to come with a strong password and a decent firewall, even though most never checked. Whenever her bot found one that could be exploited, it wrote the results to a text file that Teri maintained. It allowed her to visit each one at her leisure. By hacker standards she was a noob, a nobody with only a basic understanding of the principles she worked with. What she did know was how to spot a weakness and how to take advantage of it. Which for her purposes was more than enough.

With the text file up, Teri selected a series of related addresses and plugged them in. A new set of windows filled the screen. Four feeds from a house she had never seen before. The rooms were big, not like the cookie-cutter floor plans that popped up in subdivisions every few months. These displayed expensive taste and an astounding lack of humility. That meant one thing: Biltmore.

The level of extravagance on display existed only within the self-contained community south of city center. Typical Asheville residents belonged to the Bed Bath & Beyond set with accents from Kirkland's or Crate and Barrel. The designer drapes that adorned this home were custom-made—she recognized the fabric from her parents' interior design business growing up. The furniture was old with a high polish. A liquor cabinet sat against the far wall in the dining room, fully stocked. Who had liquor cabinets anymore? Grand but livable, the home had a familiar feel, like an artist imitating a master. The inspiration could be found across town.

A world-famous cathedral to the ostentatious, the Biltmore House had plenty of disciples in its religion of excess. A creed that urged its followers to establish a kind of commune in the southern mountains. The insulation was more than physical; residents knew they held the highest position in the city and, in particular, the city council's pecking order.

On-screen, beyond a long redwood dining table with a white linen spread, a vacant living area showed no signs of life. She pulled up the other windows, arranging them on-screen, creating a collage of surveillance to observe movements within the home. The kitchen was dark, tile gleamed in the low light from nearby windows and polished fixtures surrounded a marble island that took up most of the room.

In the front hall a heavy-looking wooden door caught her eye. A cutout and both sides featured an intricate inlay of translucent glowing panes. All the fixtures were gold or brass, cherrywood floors maybe, Oriental-style runners in the foyer.

In the garage, a recent-model Audi occupied the closest of two spaces, sparkling silver even in the darkened room. A few boxes pushed into corners, a tennis racket poking out of one, barely filled the space. On all the screens, it was quiet, no movement anywhere. No one home. She frowned. *Miss.*

Her stomach growled, impatient and ignored since breakfast. If half a microwave burrito and warm orange juice was breakfast. Her energy levels had been low that morning, unwilling to cooperate with more than a quick trip to the kitchen. As afternoon came and went, things hadn't improved. She fought the beast back with an already-opened bag of stale pretzels that lay crumpled on the desk, scattered crumbs and salt spilled from the opening. Now that the urge became painful, she knew her legs were too weak to move and, worse, the desire wasn't there. Not worth the trouble.

A life with MS was a life of ups and downs. She knew what the doctors said, what the therapist warned about as she managed the peaks, being as productive as possible when energy was high and riding out the valleys with the depression, fatigue and body aches that came with them. They meant well, but they couldn't possibly understand the toll of living day to day with an unreliable nervous system, never being certain when it would short out on her. She did the best she could, went balls out when possible and suffered the consequences. The rest she tuned out. Life wasn't meant to be lived wondering when the next attack would come and worrying about what wasn't getting done.

Malnutrition being a factor, she fought depression with a combination of caffeine, Klonopin and harmless distraction. Her entertainment was other people's lives. Lives not limited by faulty wiring but dysfunctional in their own unique ways.

A bottle of soda, neglected long enough to form a ring on the desk's wood surface, would be enough to ease the cramps that came on stronger now. It was warm, flat and disappointing, but when it hit her stomach after the initial pang, the pain subsided. The sugar and artificial sweeteners would be enough to get her muscles moving, jittery, and keep some blood flowing.

The home on-screen was a dead end, but she decided to bookmark the page and return during prime viewing hours, convinced something worth watching would happen on this feed. Rich folks had the best lives, lots of dysfunction there. Her hand hovered over the mouse, ready to click when a shadow passed through the foyer. A ghost in an empty house, gone just as fast and she paused. Someone was home. She pushed back into the leather desk chair, willing to wait it out. Another sip of soda, less bad, still awful.

"Come on out," she said.

While waiting, she turned the bottle over, picking at the label. Ragged nails chewed past the fingertips, could only shred the seam, making a mess that littered to the floor. Unlimited time and not enough energy carried a difficult life lesson. You learned how to wait. Time lumbered on, but if she was patient, life would come to her. It always did.

As time passed, a shaft of light worked its way between drawn curtain and splintered wood frame, landing on her neck, warming the skin until it burned. The focused heat forced her to slide out of the way, allowing the beam to continue its path across the room, where it landed against the far wall. At the same time every day the white arc followed a precise path through the two rooms. With a marker, she could make an urban sundial, drawing lines on the kitchen tile like Tom Hanks in *Cast Away*. She didn't need a sundial so she slid across the floor and pulled the curtain shut, returning the room to its usual gloom. The screen was no longer empty. In the hallway, seen from above, a black man in a dark suit had entered the frame.

He was large, above average height but also wide, with an official air that spoke of importance, at least perceived if not actual. The suit, which straightened his lines into crisp angles, made an immediate impact. He tugged his coat sleeves, adjusted his collar. The large man passed through the hall to the dining room, appearing on both feeds at once, then into the kitchen. She followed, intrigued. Wherever he went, he commanded attention, but he looked restless, like he was waiting for something.

The man crossed to the fridge, pulled out two bottles and set one on the counter.

... or someone.

Ch. 2

The big man popped the top on his bottle and took a swig. Teri mimicked with her own. She squirmed in her chair, legs restless, muscles jumpy, and rubbed a cramped thigh with absent focus, trained on the screen. It was time for one of those white pills, but the show had just started. The man had pulled up a stool at the counter, laptop open, fingers moving fast across tiny keys. Sometimes you had to wait.

Teri pushed her weight into the chair, stretching her aching legs. Her feet up on the desk, they brushed a stack of papers close to the edge. It only took a nudge to send a cascade of doctor's bills, rejection forms and lawyer's office correspondence into a trash bin that waited below. Her new filing system. It was enough to make her smile, and she settled in further, getting as comfortable as possible.

Outside, Traffic hit a lull as narrow streets came to a standstill. The din of downtown activity faded to a white noise, part of the ambience in the old apartment. The longer she lived downtown, the more she became accustomed to the ebb and flow of city life. At times it was loud, others overbearing. Then all became calm and evening settled in. This was the in-between when anything was still possible. The bustling activity that surrounded her haven was a comfort even if she had no real desire to interact with it. Being surrounded by other people meant that if something serious happened, if she fell in the lobby bringing back groceries, or a relapse hit that landed her in bed for a week, in theory, help wasn't far away. That assurance was part of the reason Teri's mother helped her get the place instead of moving back home. *Not a chance.*

The shoebox sized apartment was little more than a bedroom and a kitchen with space for a secondhand couch and a worn computer desk. Compact was part of the plan. Small spaces were easier to navigate with a cane and meant less to clean, which had never been her specialty and likely never would be. Pulling out the vacuum or even picking up her socks every day wasn't in the cards, but if she started a few days in advance, Teri could get the whole place in order before her mother's monthly visit. Even if it pissed her off a little more each time she couldn't manage something on her own, the illusion that she was somehow a self-sufficient, fully functional adult remained a little longer.

She was counting days, trying to remember how long since the last visit, when she realized the man was gone again. The laptop lay closed on the counter, bottles abandoned. The action had shifted to another screen. She found him in the hall, where a shadow shifted behind the decorative glass of the front door. When the man, who she thought of now as Mr. Business, opened it, a dark-haired woman in heels stepped in.

She was tall and pretty and looked younger than him by at least a decade.

"Interesting," Teri said.

Mr. Business laid a hand on the woman's back as she entered, less than romantic but more than just friends. A subtle arm grab and squeeze on her part carried more suggestion. If there was a Mrs. Business, she wouldn't appreciate that. The couple moved together to the kitchen, where Mr. B. retrieved another beer for himself and opened hers. Chivalry wasn't dead, yet.

Times like these, Teri grew frustrated with home security systems that didn't come standard with audio. They were like silent movies in full color she was forced to provide her own dialogue for. Where that failed, she developed backstories for her characters. These characters were engaged in friendly chatter with a familiar undertone. Their bodies leaned together, bridging the space. The couple were all smiles and within minutes, hands touched while they spoke. For all his size, the big man showed a practiced tenderness to his guest, mixed with good-natured laughter.

He was clean-cut in a deliberate way. A man of power and influence. His domain reached to anything within his grasp, and she figured the woman, still young in life and career, was spending plenty of time within that grasp. Having a leg up on the competition was a good thing, even if that leg was behind your head. She reasoned that a purely sexual attraction wasn't out of the question as the couple grew handsier by the minute.

The action simmered, but the boiling point was far off. She scooped up her phone from the desk. Two messages, both from Thomas.

You alive?

An hour later:

Hey pretty lady. Check in when ya can.

Thomas, her guardian angel, made sure she never went too long without human contact or slipped too far into depression, and listened when things went bad, which was often. She texted back.

`Hey man, my fault. What's shakin?`

While she waited, hand holding progressed to arm rubbing, as the woman worked her way up, gliding over expensive fabric. Teri blew up the window with a click, giving it passive attention. Her phone buzzed.

`Thomas: Checking up. All good?`
`Teri: Lemme speak to Samson.`

Samson, their private code for weed, referenced a nineties stoner flick that represented one of a million obscure features in their relationship. If Thomas was out, there was nowhere else to turn until a new batch came in.

`Thomas: You're my dealer, remember?`

She huffed.

`Teri: Ran out. No self-control.`

She put a sad face at the end, a shameless attempt to elicit sympathy. There was a longer pause this time.

`Thomas: I got you.`

She put a smile after that one and a kissy face. Far out of character, she rolled her eyes. He'd see right through her.

Every month, Teri bought a few ounces from the same website that hosted her home business. It was medical grade out of California. Since she cut back on pills, weed was the only medication she used to battle the worst symptoms. It did nothing to relieve the nausea, fatigue, persistent nerve pain or overwhelming desire to pee every ten minutes, but it made her not a give a shit about any of that, and it was an effective sedative, which was good enough.

Thomas wasn't even a recreational smoker, but he had introduced her to the Dark Web, had helped set up her store and online wallet and had taken the risk of shipping her packages until she worked out her own system. In exchange he got a little of her stash and anything else he needed at a discount. Asking for any of the paltry amount she gave him hurt her pride and made her feel irresponsible.

Teri: Text after work.

She set the phone down, returning to the action. The man was gone, but the woman remained and she wasn't sitting anymore. She was bent over the counter, laptop open, hands moving in quick strokes.

"Now what are you doing?" Teri said.

Even when she leaned in, it was difficult to make out anything on the other screen, but the woman was working fast. She reached in her purse, retrieved something small and plugged it into the computer. She had a flash drive. *Interesting.* Images flashed across the laptop screen, and the woman checked over her shoulder as she worked. She squinted at the monitor the same as Teri did watching her, trying to see the files she copied. The woman was deliberate and alert. With a jerk, she slapped the lid closed, removed the drive and slipped back into her seat just as Mr. Business reappeared. The drive slid into the woman's purse unnoticed.

Her head tilted up, a smile on her lips when the big man placed an arm around her shoulders. He rubbed her neck, shoulders and arms. Her head lolled, letting him work deep into the muscles, his massive hands kneading tender flesh. Several minutes passed as strong fingers flexed against soft skin. Something whispered in her ear brought a smile to red lips. No need to hear what when the woman rose, as if by command, and slid her stool away from the counter. Mr. Business snatched up the beer bottle beside the laptop, chugged the last bit and tossed it in the trash.

From behind, the woman couldn't see the unease that clouded his face when he passed the counter. From her vantage point, Teri saw suspicion, a tension in the muscles of his face and hands.

The woman had removed her coat, laying it across the chair, revealing bare shoulders and a sheer blouse, oblivious. When he opened the lid, frowning at the screen, she froze, recovered and took on a convincing simile of nonchalance, but her eyes went to his hands, watched them work.

He entered something that had to be a password, waited for the screen to load. The posture change was instant. From suspicion to rage, hands curled over the keys in tight fists. His head lifted, body language rigid, deliberate. The woman never budged, staring down the accusation. Teri chewed her lip. She was trying to play dumb.

Run, stupid.

Once it started, knowing how this would play out did nothing to stop it. She willed the woman to leave, begged her to get out fast, but she stood her ground, arms crossed. Not even a flinch when the laptop slammed shut.

He was around the island with surprising quickness. The woman shrank but not enough to escape a heavy hand that landed on her bare shoulder. He spoke again, imposing himself into her space. Her head shook vigorously. The confidence was gone but not the determination. The will to escape unharmed. She feigned confusion like a pro. Well enough that Teri almost believed the act.

Face hot, Teri's chest thumped in anticipation. Inches from the screen, she was sucked into the moment.

"Get out," she said, startled to hear the words from her own mouth.

The woman backed away. Mr. Business followed, encroached on her, angry hands gesturing at the laptop. The woman's eyes were wide, white all around, but still no panic. She had seen this performance before. With both hands on his chest, the woman sidestepped his advance. Careful, practiced movements that portrayed casual detachment. Her muscles were tense, but her posture was calm, assured.

It worked. The big man's shoulders slumped. He released his grip. Meaty fingers worked his temples, rubbing in slow circles. The aggression ebbed away, though the effects lingered in the air. Whatever she said, he bought it. She had soothed the beast with a dose of feminine mystique. *Performance of the year.* The woman unbuttoned the highest clasp on her blouse, wasting no time as he slid her stool under the counter.

Even in heels she had to stand on tiptoes when she sauntered closer and rose to meet his lips. She kissed him long and hard, hands clasped behind a thick muscled neck. His large fingers curled in her hair, gathering a handful of raven strands. *Way to change the subject.* The woman pressed herself close to his massive body.

In a swift move, Mr. Business closed his fist, yanked the woman's head back as far as it would go. Her face twisted in a mask of horror. Her lips parted in a silent scream. In an instant, he slammed her head into the marble. When he let go, her body slid behind the counter where only her legs stuck out, not moving.

Ch. 3

Teri screamed, or she tried to scream, but nothing came out. She gaped at the monitor, unable to look away. Her hands were shaking, but she hadn't noticed yet. *Get up, get up, get up.* She repeated the words. Words which meant nothing. A pair of legs, one heel kicked free, lay motionless. Teri's mouth rocked, squeaked, then at last, a whimper. Fingers squeezed to her palms until it hurt, she watched and waited. Time had stopped; an endless expanse, like a frozen screen until she allowed herself to blink. Even longer before she started forming questions.

What did I just see? A murder. The answer was clear, but even that was too much to process. She focused instead on a broken black heel that lay on its side. She was alone—they both were, tied together in a single twisted moment in time. When Teri came to her senses, Mr. Business had stalked off somewhere else in the house.

She swallowed, fighting a gag reflex that refused to retreat. *She's going to be alright.* It was a lie, an obvious but necessary one. Something to break the spell. The phone was in her hand before she realized she was dialing: 911, that's what people did in these situations, right? What would she tell them? What address should they dispatch to? She had no idea. *Please get up.*

Mr. Business returned, no jacket, sleeves rolled on his white shirt, which stretched taut across broad shoulders. His bald head was shiny with sweat. He knelt over the body, sinking most of his bulk from view. Well-shined shoes and tailored pants straddled the woman's splayed legs.

They rocked in rhythmic, deliberate movements. Teri slapped a hand over her mouth, turned away as she realized that he was finishing the job. She fought the urge to release her stomach's contents, powerless to prevent the horror as the brute squeezed any life that remained from the woman's body.

The battle lost, Mountain Dew and microwave burrito ejected into wastebasket. Chunky vomit splattered envelopes, dripped from the edges. Spit hung from her open mouth. Her face was hot with spots of light that danced in her vision.

It wasn't long before darkness clouded her oxygen-starved brain, where ragged breaths weren't doing the job. She leaned over the desk, waited for another retch that never came. It was minutes before she was able to regain composure and the courage to accept what she'd seen. The woman's face with that clever upturned smile, her wide innocent eyes, lingered in Teri's mind. Burned into her memory.

This time when she grabbed the phone, Teri dialed the three numbers and waited. It picked up on the second ring, a voice that was calm and professional.

"Nine-one-one. What's your emergency?"

"I ..." She stumbled, looked back to the screen. He was gone—they both were. The slender legs, laid askew on spotless tile, were missing. She searched the feeds, no activity. No one. No sign of anything. *What?*

The line hung open, a faint sound of typing on the other end.

A flash of red light in the upper corner of the screen. Taillight glare washed out the feed entirely. The rear of the car was out of frame—she couldn't see a thing.

"Nine-one-one ... please state your emergency."

The voice brought her back.

"I—I saw a murder," she said. Her voice was distant, not quite her own.

Her hands flew to the keys, hitting the combo for record. *Fuck, why hadn't she been recording?*

"Are you in danger, ma'am?"

The red light went off moments before a shadow passed through the garage, emerging in the kitchen. She spoke, not hearing her own words.

"No, I'm fine."

"Where did you see the murder?"

"I ... what?"

Her eyes couldn't leave him, entranced by his causal nature. The man was calm, unhurried, a homeowner just in from taking out the trash.

"Where did you see a murder, ma'am?"

"I ..." She searched for words. What could she say? Would it make a difference?

"I ... I made a mistake," she said.

The operator spoke again. Teri hung up.

Shit.

Wielding a towel and a spray bottle, he was on his knees, working a section of floor beyond her view. Sweat beaded on his head, which he wiped at regular intervals with a massive forearm. After the floor, he focused on the counter where a spot that must have been blood disappeared under his abrasive efforts. Within ten minutes he was drying his hands and tossing the towel in a trash can that sat beside the back door.

Teri's phone lit up while she watched. The emergency operator calling back. She flipped the phone over, ignoring the vibrations until they stopped.

In turn, he sprayed every surface in the kitchen, wiped each one until it shone. He focused extra effort on grout lines before he pulled a bucket from the closet and mopped the floor. Despite the grotesque scene, he expertly avoided tarnishing himself or his clothes. When he finished, the remaining supplies joined the towel in the trash, which he walked to the garage. Another flash of red.

She fell back, cradled in the seat, exhausted and astonished. Out of reflex she reached for the pipe, picked it up, then put it back down. Her mind railed against what it had seen, refused to accept it, absorb it. She blinked at the screen until her eyes burned; then she cried. Hot tears that streaked down her face before she could stop them. The screen, her apartment, everything blurred before she squeezed her eyes shut against it.

No no no. Think. Think.

The emergency number stopped calling. She opened her messages and typed with shaky fingers.

Call me, now.

Seconds lasted forever. Was this happening? She called Thomas.

It rang twice. A hushed voice answered.

"At work. Can't talk."

Now she broke down.

"I need your help. I need you to … can you come over? Please."

He knew her. She wasn't prone to hysterics. She never called him at work. His understanding showed in his tone.

"I'm at work. Tell me what's going on. Are you alright?"

The dam threatened to burst. She heard her voice crack.

"No. No, I'm not all right. It's not all right. I saw …" Her jaw rocked in the socket. She had to say it, to put it in words. To make it real.

"Teri …"

"I saw a murder. A man just killed somebody. On the camera … on … oh God. She's dead, man. She's fucking dead and he killed her and … I saw him do it."

Teetering, threatening to plunge into full-blown panic attack, she was scared of losing control more than anything. She sought out something, anything to distract herself from the moment. She grabbed her cane from its spot beside the desk and made her way to the window. The sprawl of downtown reminded her there was more to the world than those four walls that felt like they were closing in, more every second. She struggled to push air out of her chest, hyperventilation setting in. Thomas spoke slowly.

"What are you saying? Someone was murdered?"

Her voice was deep and ragged, still trembling.

"I saw a man, on the cameras. He killed a woman. I … think she's dead. She's probably dead." She backtracked out of wishful thinking, nothing more.

"You're not sure?"

"She's dead. I'm sure."

"But not positive?"

"Thomas!"

"What?"

"He killed her."

'Alright, Call the cops."

"I did."

Long pause.

"And?"

The scenes racing through her mind threatened to trigger another attack. Focused on controlled breathing like the therapist taught her, she spoke slowly and deliberately.

"I hung up."

The line was silent. She knew what he would say.

"I don't understand. Why would you do that? You saw a crime, Teri. You have to report that, now before it's too late."

"It's already too late. He cleaned the scene—the body is gone. There's nothing to do."

In as even a tone as she could manage, she described what she had seen, how he had sanitized the scene with methodic attention.

"There's always something. They can find stuff, stuff you'd never look for. You need to call someone and get the cops over there right now."

He was right, but there was more to consider.

"Where? Where do I tell them to go? I don't know where he lives. And if I did, how do I explain this? You don't think someone is going to want an explanation? How did I see it happen? What was I doing logged into a rich man's security system? What if they check my computer? I'll go to jail."

"Teri."

"What … ?"

"He killed someone. You have to—"

"That's it. She's dead. I'm not."

"You're serious."

"Do I have a choice?"

She was certain as soon as the words came out. She didn't have a choice here.

He cleared his throat. Dead air between them. Outside, a wide orange ribbon spread across the horizon. Sunset coming soon.

"So, then what?" he said at last.

She gathered herself. Watching life continue, oblivious to the horror she'd just witnessed.

"I don't know. I freaked out a little, but I'll figure something out. I just need a minute. Talk to me, please."

"Could you get that address if you had to?"

She thought about it.

"I don't know. It's not that easy. I'm not that kind of tech."

"Could you try?"

She sniffed, glanced over her shoulder at the screen. The screen now empty, still recording.

"Yeah, I could."

"OK, do that. I'll call you back."

The line went dead.

He didn't understand what he was asking. It was one thing to know your IPs came from a specific provider; it was another entirely to find where they were assigned. It would be impossible, but she was thankful for the task. Impossible meant it would take time, give her something to do. Maybe he knew that.

First, she needed a drink. More than anything, she needed to move, to allow her mind and body to process what had just happened.

She made her way to the kitchen, leaning more than usual on her cane arm. Stress had amplified the weakness in her legs, making it difficult to walk. They felt unsteady, unstable and yet somehow stiff. Adrenaline made her body shake until she was vibrating.

She wanted vodka or whiskey but water was free and all she had. One glass down, sitting uneasy in her stomach, halfway through another, a knock at the door broke the silence. It came loud, hard and determined.

"Mrs. Fletcher?"

Nervous fingers clutched the mug handle, her heart an erratic rhythm.

"Who is it?" she managed and regretted it at once.

"Sheriff's department, ma'am. Responding to a call."

Cell phones had address records? She should have known that. Why didn't she know that? She raced through her options. There were none.

"One minute," she called.

The dead bolt slid free with a click. The night chain rattled in its track, still engaged. She eased the door open, only a few inches. Just enough that her face and hand holding the door were visible from the outside. The dim hall light struggled to reveal a pair of stone-faced officers. The one closest to her, a man with short hair, a deep tan and cool blue eyes, watched her with curiosity when she peeked through the opening. A Hispanic woman, hair pulled tight with drawn-on eyebrows, studied every crevice of the small hallway; she seemed to notice everything except Teri.

"Mrs. Fletcher?"

He meant Joan, her mother, the name on the lease, but technically still correct.

"Yes," she said.

"We received an emergency call from this address. Is everything OK?"

He stretched to see past her to the apartment. She shifted to block his view.

"It's fine. I—I made a mistake. I'm sorry." She was pleased that the quiver in her voice had subsided to a mild shake.

His eyes narrowed like he wanted to speak, but radio chatter interrupted. The woman stepped back and spoke into a mouthpiece on her shoulder.

"Can you open the door please?" he asked.

Teri shifted her weight, moving so the cane peeked through the crack. A little sympathy never hurt.

"No, I—I'd rather not, thanks. It was a mistake. I ... just made a mistake. I'm sorry."

His face fell, disappointed.

"Do you know it's illegal to make prank calls to an emergency number?" he said.

"It wasn't a prank." She flushed. Her neck was hot. She must be sweating bullets. She could feel her shirt clinging to sweat on her back.

"I thought I saw something, but I didn't. Thanks for coming, but it's all right. Promise."

The man stayed, staring her down. Did he have probable cause? Logically, she was safe, but her chest still thumped, her nerves popping like firecrackers. She tried to swallow, but her throat scratched, sandpaper that almost made her choke. He wouldn't leave so she studied his badge. Wallace, was that a first name or last?

Officer Wallace looked over her shoulder one more time, sneered and turned to his partner. The woman shrugged, satisfied that nothing smelled funny here. Aside from the hall, which Teri knew smelled like wet dog more often than not. She focused on putting forward her most innocent face, determined there was no way a cop was entering this apartment. He relented.

"'All right. Let's be more careful from now on, huh?"

"Yessir, definitely." She nodded, forcing a weak smile.

Officer Wallace left her view. The woman cut her eyes with a thin-lipped smile. It said either "Have a nice day" or "Thanks for wasting our time." She disappeared as well, fresh radio chatter echoing down the stairwell. When the footsteps faded, Teri closed the door and clicked the dead bolt in place. She dropped to the floor, exhaling loud enough to hear outside.

"Son of a bitch," she said.

Unaccustomed to the adrenaline, muscles in her lower back seized, squeezed around her spine. It felt like her kidneys were shutting down. Nerve endings sparked like live wires. Legs extended, she allowed her head to thump against the door. She squeezed her eyes shut and wished it all away. *Please let this be a shitty dream.*

On the desk her phone buzzed.

Ch. 4

"Are you alright?" The panic in his voice was tangible. Much louder than the whisper before with more background noise also.

"Sorry, I was on the floor, took a minute to get the phone." She said

"Why were you—"

"Because the cops came, long story. I promise I'll tell you later when life isn't royally fucked."

"So ..."

"I told them to go away," she snapped.

Teri fell back into her chair, determined not to leave it again. Come hell or high water she was not going to move. She might even sleep there. Her calves and toes had started to cramp, squeezing the tendons in a vice. Once they locked up, it could be hours before they released on their own. She focused on breathing, trying to bring her heart rate down, tried to think about something positive. Thomas wanted to help—she wasn't alone.

"I'm sorry. I don't know what to do," she said.

His voice cut out, wind whipping against the microphone.

"Can you make an anonymous report? I could do it if you want."

She had considered that.

"How many murders you think happen a year? If there was an investigation, and they've already been here once? I can't."

The fact was she couldn't risk that. Her lifestyle was too questionable. A felony meant instant denial of all benefits, even the ones she had now. Once the cops got started snooping, wanted to know how she stumbled on this tragic incident, it was a short step to asking to see the recordings, confiscating the hard drive, finding her 'business.' It was too dangerous to risk her own life for someone that was already dead.

"I know, it's shitty and I'm a shitty person but no one is looking out for me right now."

Silence.

"Except for you."

"You're not shitty but we have to do something."

He sighed, disappointed but not surprised. Something told her he had expected that answer. An electric tone like a car door being held open chimed in the background.

"What are you doing?" she asked.

"Did you get that address?"

She had forgot.

"No, I was preoccupied."

"Think you can?"

"Yeah, I'm pretty sure it's Biltmore. The place is gigantic, gotta be over there somewhere."

"Excellent, I'm headed that way. Let me know when you have more."

She broke in.

"Why are you going there? There's nothing you can do."

"You can't call it in, right? We can't make an anonymous tip. Maybe if I swing by, I can see something suspicious. Probable cause, something like that. They find him before he gets rid of the evidence, no need for witnesses. This guy goes straight to jail."

It sounded good but too simple.

"Someone will put it together."

She heard the pause as he gathered himself.

"So what, forget about it, let him get away? Do you think you could live with yourself if he does it again? This way doesn't tie back to you. If anyone asks questions, just play dumb. They won't need your testimony to prosecute anything."

She thought about it. Thought about the woman, that sly grin, the scream Teri couldn't hear that would haunt her the rest of her life. A silent plea for mercy, followed by a swift and violent denial.

"I'll work on it."

"Hit me up if you find something. I'll call you when I'm close."

They had two developments to choose from. Biltmore Forest and Biltmore Shores. Biltmore Forest was older, built on the original mansion grounds, a sprawl of old money with a massive golfing green at the center. The gargantuan homes came with multimillion-dollar price tags and instant prestige, but they had all been built in the early days when real estate was cheap and classic architecture was in style. They were grand but dated.

Biltmore Shores was a new development, a decade old at best, with many of the mini-mansions constructed more recently than that. Teri eyed the interior shots spread across the monitor. The lines were modern, the ceilings lower than their Victorian-inspired counterparts across town. These floors glowed, not yet showing signs of age, but the deciding factor was the glass inlay collecting sun in the wide front door. Bold, elegant and slightly abstract, it had a contemporary feel that spoke of new construction. She sent a message to Thomas.

`Biltmore Shores.`

It was a guess. One based on observation and instinct, but she was confident. Maybe there were new homes in both divisions—maybe she was completely off base, but her gut said to go with it, so she did. There might be a hundred homes in Biltmore Forest. At the Shores there were maybe twenty, spread along a narrow strip of reengineered lakefront shoreline. She liked her odds and said a silent prayer they would come up in her favor.

Teri pulled up Maps online and zoomed in on the area.

"Now … which one are you?"

These rooftops took up three times the real estate of others in the city. Each one situated on an acre or more of land. Most houses had semicircle driveways, almost all with an attached garage. She needed more. Since it would take Thomas about fifteen minutes to get across town, she figured that meant about a minute each to eliminate some options.

With nothing of value outside, she turned to the inside. The kitchen could be avoided, which allowed her to put that scene out of her mind a little longer. She needed something specific, something unique and visible from the street. She scanned each window with a discerning eye and landed again on the stained glass. It caught the evening sun, causing brilliant red, green and yellow panes to light up the wall, patterns cast throughout the foyer until the space was a kaleidoscope of colors. That window was key to picking this house out of the crowd. If she could find it.

Switching to street view, she moved at painstaking speed, frame by frame through the neighborhood, searching for the ostentatious glass. Her fingers tapped the desk, growing more impatient with each click. One by one, each street came to a dead end. Too many homes set too far back, obscured by well-trimmed boxwoods or not visible at all. She checked the time, seven minutes gone already. No time to look at every one. *New Plan.*

What else?

She returned to the foyer. The evening sun created a lens flare that made it impossible to discern any kind of pattern in the glass. While she searched, trying to pick out the details, *he* appeared again. His body blocked the light where he stood to check the front door, cocked his arm to reveal an expensive-looking watch and left the frame again toward the kitchen. She kept him in her peripheral as he went to work on something in the kitchen but strained to keep herself on task.

The living room and the dining room went nowhere. No clues that could lead her or Thomas to the scene. Nothing stood out. Two windows faced the street that would be indiscernible from any other in the same neighborhood. A door to a patio on the far wall pointed the wrong direction to be seen. There were two windows in the dining room, tall, dressed with expensive curtains and thick blinds. By the halo that appeared now, she guessed another row of windows ran beneath the camera mount. She chewed her lip.

"Come on."

Half desperation, half intuition landed on a shaft of pure white light that worked its way across the living room. Brilliant on the thick white carpet, it halted just short of a white designer sofa. The entire living room lit like a cathedral , filling the space with divine providence.

Of course.

All that light came from the west. That at least meant this house had to be facing west also to catch this much sun late in the day. She slid the camera feed to the top of the screen, sharing space with Maps. From the aerial view, it was easy to see that at least two-thirds of the homes in the Shores faced north or northeast, positioning their back lots along the longest lakeshore. She counted out the handful of west-facing lots. Only five matched.

The phone rang.

"Yeah?" she said.

"Hey, hang on a second."

Rustling filled the earpiece, followed by a distant masculine voice. When Thomas spoke, the tinny echo told her he had her on speaker, eavesdropping on his conversation.

"Here to see Mr. Smith," Thomas said with confidence.

The deep voice spoke again—she couldn't make it out. Something like "pass," maybe "fast." He sounded unpleasant.

"I don't know. He's my dad's friend," Thomas said. He must be at the guardhouse, trying to talk his way in. The two men went back and forth while she scrolled through options on-screen searching for something to give him if it worked.

"Sorry, no. He didn't tell me. I'm supposed to pick up golf clubs or something. I don't know, man."

She listened, passive. Thomas was many things, but he wasn't afraid to take a risk now and then. When time came for boldness, she knew he'd be the last to shy away. He took it as a challenge.

The other end was garbled, but the words "Turn around" stood out in a field of noise.

"Help me out, bro, come on. My dad's gonna be pissed if I don't take care of this. Here, take my license, I'll leave it here."

A pause.

"I dunno, Phil or something. Hook me up, man."

She heard the motor rev.

The sound changed again. Now his voice was clear, close.

"Shit," he said.

"No go?"

"Hell no. Doesn't seem like a brown people kind of neighborhood," he said.

She eyed the big man taking his place at the counter. Hunched over the screen again.

"I think it's a money thing."

"All right, poor brown people. You didn't see the look he gave me."

"Fair enough, but you tried, so let's forget it. We'll come up with something else."

She heard a blinker clicking over the speaker. No response.

"Thomas?"

"I'm gonna park down the street. I think there's another way in."

"Thomas."

"What …"

She listened to dead air as Thomas cased the street.

In the garage, the body of a young woman was curled up in the trunk of that silver Audi. Still, in the tomb-like space. Her skin grew cold in a casket of steel and premium synthetic fibers. It made Teri's jaw clench; she was angry at the man who put her there, angry at herself for being the only chance this poor woman had at justice. She pulled out a notepad and drew a quick diagram of the rooms she had access to.

It wasn't very useful. An L-shaped pattern with too much unexplored. A west-facing house like any other, garage to the side. It could be any house on the street. She had an unfinished maze lacking definition.

"Shit!" She slammed her hand on the desk hard enough it hurt.

"What happened?" Thomas asked. Concern filled his voice. She forgot he was on the line.

"I can't find it," she said. "I think I have the street, but that's it. I can't figure out which one it is."

"That's a start. Which street is it?" he said.

"Julian. It's south of the front gate on the lake near the back. There's some docks with boats and stuff."

"Perfect, I found a way in. The fence line stops at a little grove of trees back here. I bet you there's a path down to the lake. I can walk the shoreline, maybe get in that way."

That sounded reasonable and dangerous.

"Please, be careful."

"Always. Let me call you back. Keep looking, you're doing great."

The line went dead again. She envied his confidence, especially how much he had in her. It was completely unfounded, but he never wavered in his absolute faith that Teri was in control of every situation. He was wrong. More often than not, she was winging it with a grin and a prayer, but he chose to ignore that, and she was thankful, even if she wasn't good at showing it.

Out of ideas, she watched, waiting for clues to present themselves. Sometimes you had to let life come to you. Mr. Business sat at the counter, laptop open. His hands moved in brisk strokes across the keys. Was he deleting more evidence? A fresh bottle sat at his side and she wished more than anything for one of her own. She would sit across the bar from him, brew in hand, and wait for the cops to arrive.

Her phone buzzed.

`Thomas: I'm in, what am I looking for?`

She full-screened the hallway monitor and took a picture, sent it to him with a note.

`Teri: This door. It's all I've got. Four windows, facing west.`

She pulled up the map and typed out the addresses she had, sent that in another message. As she hit Send, the front door opened. A teenage girl, maybe fifteen, came in, dropped a backpack and headed down the hall directly under the camera.

`Teri: Kid just came home. Look for a school bus. Maybe some teenagers driving.`

She stared at the screen, no response.

The girl had disappeared, but Mr. Business closed the laptop. He finished the beer, tossed it and began pulling containers from the fridge. For the next hour, the big man and his daughter prepared dinner. They chatted at the counter, the one he had murdered a woman at only hours ago. A woman who was still stuffed in a trunk in the garage while they boiled spaghetti. He chopped vegetables like it didn't still smell of bleach, where her blood had sprayed. She watched him share a meal with the young girl, who sat in the same high-backed chair the woman had when she'd winked at the bastard, promising more to come. He patted the girl's hair when she squeezed by to drop her empty dish in the sink.

Teri: Hey, you alive?

Another thirty minutes disappeared while the girl curled up on the couch, feet tucked under, tapping away at her phone. Thin but tall, she folded up on herself like a baby giraffe. At five ten, Teri was tall for a woman, and this girl could almost look her in the eye. She obsessed over her. Whether she suspected what her father was capable of. Was she safe? Most of all, she wondered where the mother was. Maybe another victim. Those thoughts were easier than focusing on the increasing time elapsed since she'd heard from Thomas. The last message still unanswered.

The shaft of light was gone, absorbed into the gathering shadows. The young girl sat under a lamp on a wooden end table, thumbs working at furious speed. Teri's apartment had grown dark except for the blue glow of the computer screen. She adopted the girl's posture, balling up in the office chair. Her legs ached but her stomach had given up its protests.

Panic didn't set in until after eight thirty. Now over three hours since his last message. When her calls went directly to voice mail, she left two messages and sent angry texts. She sent worried texts. His Facebook said he hadn't signed on since yesterday.

Teri: You better be dead.

She hit Send, felt bad about it.

Teri: Please don't be dead. What happened … are you alright?

The girl's head jerked to the foyer and then over her shoulder down the hall. A moment later the man came through, no longer dressed in suit and tie. Now in cargos and a T-shirt, he was a decent imitation of the average man. On the hall cam, shadows lurked beyond the glass-paned door. When it opened, a pair of uniformed officers stepped in.

Ch. 5

Two men entered. One took a place in the hall between rooms. The other remained in the doorway. These weren't sheriffs like the two she encountered. They were wearing city uniforms. The first man was older with silver-flecked hair. He took charge from the start. Mr. Business ordered the girl away with a wave of his hand. She took the order immediately but sat again when the older officer addressed her directly.

Teri blew up the screen, wary but excited. It didn't matter how these men got there. If they made it to the garage, her problems were over. Miracles *could* happen. She texted Thomas again.

Teri: Are you seeing this? Cops at the house, right now. Where are you?

The three men spoke in the foyer. Unclear body language, words she couldn't hear or lip-read. Everyone was calm, professional. The older man, who appeared to be the lead, proved her theory when he took Mr. Business to the side. They walked to dining room, heads bowed, the officer rolling a hand in the air, an explanation unfolding. One Mr. Business accepted without a hint of emotion. He took it in, nodding when called for.

The younger man posted himself in the front hall, thumbs hooked in his belt. He looked like a cowboy in blue polyester.

Large paws resting on his hips, Mr. Business listened, squinted as the officer spoke. He showed no agitation, made no attempt to interrupt. As they spoke, at all times, he appeared interested and attentive to what the officer had to say. It was fascinating how his eyes narrowed, his brow creased, in time with what he heard.

The man was practiced at deception. His easy mannerisms were a contrast to the straight posture and serious expression of the officer. When at last the man offered a sweeping hand of acceptance, inviting the officer to have a look around, she thought he darted a glance to the girl still sitting on the sofa, but it was too quick, over in an instant.

For his part, once the officer motioned for Mr. Business to join his daughter in the other room, he took pains not to come in contact with anything in the home. Hands behind his back, the man eased into the kitchen, covered the space with a scrutinizing glare. He leaned forward, pointing with his nose like a bloodhound when he peered under the counter's edge, nudged the stool to the side with a polished shoe. When he crouched in the same space where the woman had lain for the last time, he was for a moment hidden from view, Teri realized she was holding her breath. She inhaled quick and sharp. She forced herself to take long metered breaths. Her fingers clenched.

The man emerged and hovered over the counter edge. She hadn't told Thomas about that. About the spray of blood from the woman's nose before she went down. Did he see something? She found herself chanting. *Yes, yes, yes.* Trying to nudge fate to will his recognition of a crime being covered up. She almost shouted when he spoke into his radio and stopped to listen before turning his back on the room. Eyeing the space that would be the end of Mr. Business, he moved on to the garage door.

The man paused. Something shouted over his shoulder got attention in the living room. The backup addressed Mr. Business who nodded approval. Once he received clearance via more shouts, the older officer pulled a cloth from his pocket, turned the handle and eased down the steps.

The light switch was on the kitchen side. When flipped, it lit up the room in a fluorescent glow. For the first time she saw the space for what it was, a two-car garage with only one space occupied. The Audi took up most of the frame. Beyond that, there was a series of shelving units against a far wall, cardboard boxes shoved into corners, a workbench that looked rarely, if ever, used. It appeared unremarkable and underutilized, but her focus and the officer's landed on the same location.

High-gloss paint reflected a distorted version of the well shined black shoes and the glint of metal from his gun belt as the officer circled the car. He shone a flashlight underneath, kneeling beside polished rims. Traced the light along the wheel wells and the windows and gave special attention to a wide area on all sides of the car. When he flicked off the flashlight, he circled behind the car and disappeared from view. Moments later he appeared on the other side and went directly for the steps up to the kitchen.

Teri clenched and opened her fist, scratching at the nubs of her nails. Why wasn't he checking the trunk? They *had* to check the trunk. Hadn't they been tipped off? Wasn't anything suspicious always in the trunk?

She turned to the second-floor window, distracted by noise outside. The streetlights were on; crowds began to form downtown. Her skin crawled with adrenaline like she'd popped a handful of Adderall on an empty stomach. Raw energy coursed through her veins. She pleaded with the screen.

"Look in the car. *Look in the car!*"

Her fists slammed onto the desk.

"Come on."

They reconvened in the living room. The officer brought a chair from the dining room, set it across from the girl on the sofa. Her father took up the space to her side. The backup kept his position except now he leaned against the doorframe. Teri ground her teeth, infuriated by the silence. What were they saying? Where were the handcuffs?

The figure in the living room remained passive, relaxed. Not a man facing murder charges. He was a man who had set his mind to letting things progress as they would, confident in his own ability to escape prosecution.

One hand rested in his lap; the other, across the back of the sofa, hung limp on his daughter's shoulders. The implication clear; possession. He had one leg crossed over, like a man entertaining old friends, except for the badges and guns.

The girl was more energetic, fidgety to a noticeable degree. Her fingers never left her phone screen even when the officer spoke to her. Her eyes rarely lifted and they never faced her father.

Teri's own palms stung where her nails had cut half-moons in the tender flesh. She laid them flat in her lap, calming herself. The cops were there; they knew something had happened. She had to wait and let them do their job. Her own phone was silent. No new messages. *Where could he be?*

The charade continued for too long until the younger cop came to attention. At once he went to the door, stepped outside and returned a moment later with a short, dark-haired woman in tow. Her hair in a ponytail, wearing street clothes, she carried a small silver box that could have been a tackle box or a large makeup case. Around her neck hung a camera with a large barrel lens. Behind her, a man in a suit flashed a badge at the door and followed the woman into the house.

Mr. Business leaned forward, no longer at ease. He leered at the new guests, ready to object. The older officer faced him, spoke a few words. Teri wished she'd heard them, because he frowned, leaned back again, but never took his eyes off the woman with the silver case.

Without further objection the older officer joined the newcomers in the dining room with gestures toward the kitchen and beyond that looked like instructions.

He had called a detective, and she guessed the woman to be a crime-scene investigator. The pair took over and moved into the kitchen. The older officer returned to his chair in the living room, babysitting the suspect, while the backup held up the doorframe, looking bored. She noted that he never made eye contact with anyone else in the room.

On a side counter the woman set down her case and flipped the latches. Inside were several bottles of various sizes and an array of items too far away to make out. Teri did recognize a pair of white gloves and a spray bottle with clear liquid, which the woman set to the side. The pair worked quick, in unison. The detective directed the woman to areas of the scene, where she snapped photos, some far away, others close. Each time, she took notes on a small pad in her pocket. After several dozen photographs, she let the camera hang and slipped on the latex gloves as the detective flipped off the overhead light. The screen went black.

In the dark, only huddled shapes were visible, their outlines catching light from the other rooms but too indistinct to make out their actions. Even when Teri leaned close, the room was inky black, too dark to make anything out.

When the light returned, the woman replaced the spray bottle in the kit and turned the camera where the detective could see the LCD screen. He shook his head, pointed to the display and frowned. Teri's eyebrows knit. What did they see?

Repositioning, the woman held the camera so it would be seen against the backdrop of the marble counter, the same place the blood spray had been.

Luminol! They were testing for blood.

"Gotcha now, bitch."

The process stretched on, both pointing out specific spots, comparing them with the camera screen. Teri's knee banged the underside of the desk; she was too wired to sit still. Too wound up to watch the entire song and dance before the finale. Satisfied, the woman packed her kit and followed the detective, who led the way down into the garage. They repeated the same steps as before. This time Teri knew what they were looking for, and she cheered them on as they scoured every inch of the concrete surface. Her anxiety peaked when they circled near the rear of the car. It was *right there*. They processed the scene and then cut the lights.

Look in the trunk, look in the trunk, look in the trunk, she chanted in a whisper. She praised Thomas for coming through. It was a superpower. Somehow, he always found a way. When his phone charged and he got back in touch, she had to tell him so.

When the lights came on again, the woman retrieved the notebook, taking quick notes as she followed the detective around the Audi. She addressed the detective, then packed the light and the spray bottle back into their compartments. *Check the fucking trunk!*

They lingered. The woman stood by while the detective made a second inspection of the garage. He kicked a cardboard box, pushed it across the floor. More conversation. *What are you doing? Open the trunk.*

The detective poked his head through the door, called something that got attention in the living room. She saw the backup look to Mr. Business, who stood and walked to the kitchen. He pulled a set of keys off the wall and passed them to the detective. Then he returned to the living room and retook his seat, displeased but restrained. He could play it cool with the best of them, but even this man didn't have the audacity to watch what was about to happen.

"Go for it, follow your gut," Teri said.

The detective unlocked the car with a flash of headlights. The search began again, the woman taking the driver's side. No space went unexamined, the steering wheel, the backseat, under the seats. They scoured every inch with bare eyes followed by black light. They found nothing of course because he had never been inside the car. Not since the murder. The woman took what looked like a lint roller to the seats and floor mats. Again, nothing. They closed it up.

"Come on. You're so close."

The lights flashed again, red lights in the back as the detective hit the release button for the trunk.

Yes! Thank God.

The pair disappeared from frame while Teri clutched the chair arm, waiting for the inevitable discovery. Though the rear of the car was hidden, the interior light from the open trunk was visible on-screen. It remained lit for what could have been forever. Her heart thumped. It ached, overworked and exhausted. When the interior light went out, the woman appeared first, notebook in hand. Behind her the detective followed, a hand on the woman's back as they filed back into the kitchen. They chatted the whole way, expressions flat. Something was wrong. The woman with the silver case and black hair left the house, the detective taking a place in the living room with Mr. Business and the others.

No, no, no.

The action was too relaxed, too routine. Something was definitely wrong with this scene. The older officer stood first. He brushed a pants leg, smoothed the wrinkles and listened while the detective spoke. Head bowed, the detective shook his hand, nodded to the man on the couch and reached into his coat. He retrieved a card, handed it to the girl and turned to leave. The backup officer followed his lead as far as the door.

An ice pick hit her heart as she realized what was happening. In no time everyone except the girl was gone or in the doorway.

The last to leave, the backup officer approached Mr. Business. No sound necessary to recognize a friendly chat, perhaps an apology, complicit smiles on their faces. This time the handshake was familiar, casual. A pat on the back from the huge mitt of the big man, and then the last officer turned, waved good-bye to the girl, who ignored him, and left. Mr. Business shut and locked the door behind him and punched a code into the number pad on the wall. With the wave of a rigid finger, the girl was off the couch and headed down the hall.

Teri was stunned.

For the first time the man looked agitated. He made his way to the kitchen, scowled at the empty space as his massive frame leaned on the counter. Teri glared at the screen, hating him with a sudden fierceness. She wanted something horrible to happen to him. She wanted him to get caught, to die on that floor from a heart attack. She wanted the universe to be set right, but it wasn't going to happen. Not tonight. However he had pulled it off, he was getting away with this and it seared her soul to watch. It clawed at her from the inside, powerless to change anything.

When his head turned, slow and deliberate, it froze her in place. Eyes white like a shark breaching the surface, narrow pupils looked right through her. The stare so cold, in a primal way that it made her back away from the screen. He never looked away as he dragged a stool across the tile, climbed on top and met her face-to-face. His features were a mask with no room for humanity within. One she was convinced would come through the screen when a large hand appeared and obscured her view. The screen went black.

He killed all the feeds. Confronted with darkness, Teri scrubbed back and forth over hours of footage. In darkness she watched a documentary of reactions missing one crucial scene. After the third time through, she gave up, resigned to failure. With no word from Thomas and no way to follow the action, she was in the dark.

If he was at the police station, even if he gave a statement, that had been hours ago. She would have heard something. He would have found a way to get a message to her. Thomas was Mr. Reliable, always there where and when he said he'd be. His sudden absence made her more nervous than she wanted to admit. If something happened to him, it was her fault.

Nothing else to do, she paced in the small area between her desk and the window, making sharp U-turns with weight on the cane until her wrist hurt. Her lip was chewed ragged. The darkness, so often comforting, closed in tighter than ever. The glow of the screen beckoning.

Pulling back the curtain allowed the shimmering lights of downtown into her private space. One of two windows on this wall, the other in the bedroom, it allowed her to observe the flow of crowds as they traveled to and from bars and nightclubs. Even on a weeknight, half a dozen couples strolled the sidewalk. They moved from one halo to another, secure in the streetlight. Unlike in larger cities, no one here just disappeared. She frowned. Something had to be done.

Rubbing tired eyes, she flicked on a desk lamp near the monitor and fell into her seat. The address was key. Without it, she was powerless. With it, she was still powerless but armed with crucial knowledge. It was as good a place as any to start. Fingers hit the keys as she settled in, intent on figuring out which home in this compound had a secret to tell.

She had five options to choose from. That was something. The half-drawn floor plan was useless, but she slid it to the side. It might come in handy later. From a quick survey, none of the homes were visible from street view, but the aerial image showed more than she had noticed earlier. In the backyard of one of her targets, the farthest from where Thomas would have entered, a blue kiddie pool and a swing set cast an angled shadow toward the lake. The teenager that had been on camera was much too old for that, and she'd seen no evidence of a younger child. Good enough. That left four.

Street view had failed for finding the window, but you could search older images as well if you set the date finder back to a year or even more. Cross-checking the addresses, she had now revealed a white-haired old man, liver-spotted complexion, probably late sixties. He'd stopped at the end of a driveway, the second on her list, hand raised waving at the camera car as it passed. He looked pleasant, someone's grandfather on the way to check the mail. Nothing like Mr. Business. Nothing evil in his appearance. None of the homes in the Shores were old enough to be on second owners yet. She marked it off.

That left three. Three potential addresses for her killer and, she hoped, an explanation for what had happened to her friend. The answer was there. Thomas had figured it out; now it was her turn.

Armed with three addresses and a disproportionate amount of optimism, she turned to a search engine for the rest of the puzzle. Entering each one might reveal a list of potential leads. News articles, sale ads, even yard sales on social media sites, might have something she could use. When the addresses themselves returned nothing, she tried variations, entering keywords that might boost results. She entered the address with the trailing words "Asheville," "Biltmore" and "Biltmore Shores." Nothing.

Fingers tapped on keys. Thinking. Somewhere in this mountain of information was an answer. She just had to ask the right question.

The question that rattled in her brain was why two people, one of them clearly not the homemaker type, lived in a house so large it needed its own zip code. She thought the answer might be obvious—appearances for appearances sake—but there was something else. This man had money and he liked to show it off. He was too big to have an inferiority complex, so there was something else, something pathological. Maybe flaunting his wealth was another way to impose his will on others.

She also figured that desire was a clue to his weakness. When he was challenged, the reaction came swift and merciless. Using that might work to her advantage. If she could find him.

If you want to find the root of evil, follow the money. It had been months since she'd used it but Teri remembered the city tax assessor kept a database of all homes within city limits with information on property value, taxes owed and names on the deed.

The site came up in seconds: a simple database with a basic interface on top. She navigated to a search page, found the option to search by address, typed in the first one from the list and hit Enter.

The page froze, trying to process the command on ancient government servers. Her eyes went wide as soon as the results came. A complete rundown of everything the city had on the owner. There was a button for photos, she hit that and the screen filled with a picture of this address taken from the driveway.

"Got you," she said.

She clicked back and scanned the results, learning what she could about the family that lived at 7000 Julian Circle. The home was a five-bedroom with a two-car garage, constructed only seven years ago. Estimated home value was $2,200,000. Her jaw dropped open on its own when she read it.

The website had the owner as Nancy Klein. She was current on her taxes and had paid for the past five years. Her man didn't feel like a Nancy, even if it would explain his temper. She moved on.

The second address listed Roman Gardner as the owner. Approximate value $2.25 million. Taxes were current, paid for seven years. That would make Roman one of the original residents of Biltmore Shores and would make his daughter about eight or nine when they moved in. Making this what the social elite would consider a starter home. She typed the name in Google.

Most of the results were misspellings, partial hits and one stage actor from decades ago. She refined the search to include the word "Biltmore" and then "Asheville." On that string the first result sent a chill through her veins despite the simmering fear and hatred.

Asheville Criminal Law Attorney: P. Welch, H. Lawson, R. Gardner

She offered a silent prayer and clicked the link. A header with three men in suits in a wood-paneled office flashed used-car-salesman smiles for the camera. The one on the left, looking content, confident, even handsome, confirmed her fears. Down the page under the heading "Partners," the bio boasted that Roman Gardner had gone to school at NC State, had twenty years experience with criminal law and was a member of an impossible number of committees and organizations. The details blurred together even as the implications set in.

He looked relaxed, as usual, but much younger. He had hair then, not close shaved like it was now. She searched his eyes, his smooth brow, his cocksure grin, for signs of menace. There was none. In fact, he was attractive, charismatic in a non-threatening way. She wondered, had he killed anyone yet?

Back on the search engine, she re-entered his name and scanned the results it returned. Halfway down was a link to a popular social media site. She clicked that one, greeted immediately by a private-page banner. Of course. The only information available was a set of photos he used for the profile pic and his college history, which she knew.

She clicked on the photos. Roman Gardner posed on the beach with his daughter. She was younger, maybe twelve or thirteen. A deep blue ocean filled the background. Gardner hid behind a pair of black shades. The girl smiled, rows of braces glinting in the sun. He looked every bit a loving father and the girl completely comfortable with his massive arm around her shoulders. But appearances could be deceiving. She closed the picture and ignored the next one, identical to the one from the law firm's website.

She backed out of the site. On the results page she switched to "News," hoping to find something that would give her more information about Roman Gardner. The first headline caught her attention.

Asheville Attorney Seeks Election to Court of Appeals

No way.

She clicked the link. The article detailed Roman Gardner's "continued dedication" to upholding the letter of the law, his "tireless efforts" toward improving the community and his "excellent reputation" among his peers.

At once a throbbing that hadn't been there before found root in her temples. She skimmed the rest of the article, glossing over flowery praise of Gardner and his immaculate track record. At the bottom, before she closed the window, a new link caught her attention. Under the "Related Stories" header was a headline:

Lawson/Gardner Cleared in Corruption Probe

"Hello."

She clicked the link to a new article.

Following months of investigation into the alleged misconduct of someone(s) within the law offices of Welch, Lawson & Gardner, two principal suspects, Harold Lawson and Roman Gardner, have been cleared of all charges by the district attorney's office. In a statement to the press on Tuesday, Amber Clark, assistant to the DA, said that all charges had been dropped and no further prosecution would be considered at this time.

Lawson and Gardner were under investigation after unnamed informants alerted authorities to activities that they claimed swung the decisions of critical cases in the office's favor, presumably in exchange for monetary compensation.

Lawson issued a statement early in the proceedings, calling the charges "unfounded" and comparing the accusations to "character assassination." Gardner, who remained silent during the ordeal, issued a statement saying, "I'm glad we can put all this behind us. These charges are ridiculous and the evidence nonexistent."

The article was dated five months prior. In April, Gardner was being fitted for an orange jumpsuit. By September he had his eye on a black robe.

Now Teri's head pounded, early signs of a migraine coming on. The harsh light of the monitor only made it worse, compounded by the reality of the situation. Soon the nerves behind her right eye would scream until she buried her head in darkness and maybe she would scream herself. There was more to discover, information to gather, but it had to wait. She knew who he was, and it was worse than she feared but that didn't mean he could get away it. No matter how powerful this man might be, it was up to her to make sure he saw justice. She winced. *In the morning.*

With a sneer, she closed the page and turned off the monitor. An overdue stretch elongated stiff muscles until her body was a long, tall tower of pain. Stretching up and away, tired fingers reached for a ceiling they could almost touch. When she relaxed, they recoiled, loosened, synapses reluctant to fire. Her nervous system came back online even though her entire body was on auxiliary power. Time for bed, even if that meant staring into darkness for hours trying to make sense of what had happened and what to do next. She snatched up her phone. The battery blinked a warning, a flashing five percent icon. Still no messages.

Ch. 7

It was the luminol that stuck in her mind. She lay in bed as faint blue light crept around the edges of drawn curtains. Her phone hung over her face, glowing in the dim room. The alarm was set for eight a.m., still thirty minutes to go. She had scrolled through blogs, forensics sites and news articles for over an hour. The latest one parroted what several others had said. There were many ways to avoid luminol detection and even confuse the results. Because of that, luminol wasn't considered a reliable indicator and was used a lot less often than TV crime shows had you believe. What those other sites hadn't said was how. Now she read that common household chemicals could do the job.

Cleaning agents with active oxygen components can have the effect of eliminating detection of blood and other fluids via the standard luminol test employed by most law enforcement agencies.

A lawyer would know that, of course he would. A criminal lawyer would know all the details on how to avoid detection for a crime. He would know the process and he would be familiar with what evidence was permissible and what wasn't. He would probably go along with an investigation if he knew there was no chance of finding incriminating evidence at the scene. Better to play the willing participant than become a suspect.

She cursed and slammed her fist into the blankets. It made her palm sting and rocked the mattress, which only reminded her how bad she had to pee. At the moment her legs were dead. More than just weights, they were cold and stiff like a cadaver from the waist down. Not too far from the mark, honestly. Hours of staring at the phone meant her eyes burned and her head still throbbed, though better than before. One pleasant side effect of the Ambien she took for insomnia was the few moments of blissful peace when all the pain in her body ebbed away just before she fell into unconsciousness. It was the best fifteen minutes of the day. Now that morning had arrived, the aches and pains of every day life crept in again.

Despite the drugs, sleep had been short and restless. She smelled sweat, her own. Time to get up and face the long day ahead. Self-doubt dawned like the sun that grew brighter by the second. Unwilling to wait any longer, her bladder spasmed and Teri swung her legs out, landing bare feet on cold floor. The chill intensified the urgency, but she hobbled quick as possible on stilt legs to the bathroom, racing her own body, grabbing the edges of furniture on the way for support.

Thomas hadn't responded during the night. He hadn't responded, either, to her early morning text before even garbage truck drivers had left their lots. It was quiet in the dark when she pulled up a map of Roman's neighborhood, studied the routes in and out of the gated community where her best friend had disappeared. She had found the road he told her about and discovered it was the only way to bypass security without getting noticed. A narrow strip of shoreline that ended where the neighborhood began was wide enough to swing around and come out in a row of lake-facing backyards.

Despite many reservations, she was energized to get started, to do something. Waiting made her feel like a spectator, and the implication started to chew at her conscience like rats in a crawl space. As she crossed the bedroom on the return trip, she thought adrenaline alone might be enough to push her through the worst of it, and from there inertia could take over and carry her to the finish line. But that meant she had to conserve energy now. She had to keep herself from getting worked up.

The ride share app said someone could be at her place in thirty minutes. She sat on the bed, pulled on her pants and selected a pair of slip-on shoes. Tying took effort and time, neither of which could be spared. She allowed herself to think forward to the plan, how crazy it was, how irresponsible. Even after an entire night to think it over, the idea was absurd. Unfortunately, in the depths of darkness, where brilliant ideas have a tendency to form, nothing else came. No matter how long she waited. "He would do it for you" was all the darkness had to say.

In the living room she grabbed a black canvas roll from a shelf and her keys from the desk along with a bottle of pills. Coffee was waiting, thanks to a timer on the machine, but time was short and a few sips was all she managed before a text said the driver was downstairs. Fifteen after. He was early.

The cane thumped each stair on the way down. It was a tempo she had grown used to. *Thump, slide, thump, slide* as the padded tip hit and her shoe brushed the tile. It was her theme song and every bit as ominous as those of Jaws or Darth Vader, at least to her. The strategy was to maintain the energy levels that were highest in the morning. Pacing herself, that allotment could last until midafternoon. She would make little concessions along the way and only as needed.

The building had an elevator, which was comforting when she confronted the prospect of climbing two double flights back to her floor, but going down was easy. The uneasiness that caused her knees to buckle every other step could be attributed to nerves; they would straighten up soon enough.

Truth was, the elevator was old and rusty and Teri was unequivocally claustrophobic. Stress had the worst effect of all on her condition, making her whole system shut down when prolonged, and her current situation was enough to tip those scales already. Sometimes, you had to pick your battles.

The driver, behind tinted glass in a new black SUV, scowled at the dash when she emerged into the cool morning air ten minutes later. She caught his discontented frown before he saw her approach. As soon as she stepped into the parking lot, his expression changed, a sudden overhaul of character at the site of a cane and a pronounced limp.

Out of the car with a flash, he ran around and opened her door, letting her take the shotgun spot. He waited until she lifted herself into the seat and closed the door for her. He was back around to his side in no time.

"Thank you," she said.

"Where we headed?" he asked, strapping a seat belt across his chest and shifting to gear.

"Biltmore Shores," she said.

Daryl, the driver wasn't much for conversation, which was fine. After several false starts that ranged from sports to weather and thankfully skirted around politics altogether, he turned up the radio. They spent the remainder of the trip in relative silence with a soundtrack of heavy metal mixed with awkward rap lyrics. She didn't listen to the music. Neither did she want to speak to the driver, who made frequent sideways glances at her legs and the cane that rested beside them. She wanted to think about what lay ahead and try to prepare herself. She needed the time to get her nerves together.

The ten-minute ride felt twice as long. Entering the highway, she watched the city glide by, disappear behind trees and become a hidden valley somewhere in the distance. Thick rows of pine, oak and elm obscured everything beyond their tree line. This highway sat at the tail end of the Blue Ridge Parkway, an annual attraction to leaf watchers up and down the East Coast. Millions of broad leaves showed the first indication of shifting to the blazing orange, yellow and red spectacle that drew enthusiasts by the carload. In the early stages, they were still a sickly yellowish green, the threat of full on tourist-attraction not yet realized.

South of the city, a tree-covered ridge rose on one side, an expanse of uninterrupted forest on the other. Somewhere in that valley was Biltmore Estate. The grounds had once totaled 125,000 acres. Now the mansion stood on a paltry 8,000, or about ten square miles. The estate housed a winery, two luxury hotels and a miniature village full of shops and restaurants like a tiny Appalachian Disney World. All this was on the tour. Every child visited the infamous residence at least once growing up, either on a school trip or a family outing. Teri had done both.

The SUV came off the highway to a grand oasis of shopping centers, movie theaters and dining options. The development felt like entering a new city, a well-fed, overindulged version of the one she was used to. Up close, the Vanderbilt vision was one of insulation. From society, from the city itself and from ordinances that offended higher sensibilities, all tinged with the exclusivity of the Biltmore name.

She ignored the monstrosity and directed the driver to a side street one block down from the Biltmore Shores security gate. Driving past that entrance would be a reminder that she should have taken this trip herself yesterday. It passed out of view now as they turned into the alley, high hedgerows boxing them in from either side. The road itself was little more than an access lane to an abrupt dead end at a turnaround surrounded with trees and untended shrubbery. There might have been a footpath leading into the wilderness.

A black Camry parked against the curb, red sticker on the driver-side glass, was obvious as soon as they turned in. She didn't need to see the AB sticker fixed on the back glass to know it was his. A river of ice that ran through her veins brought with it unexpected tears, which she blinked back before they could interfere. There was still no evidence that anything criminal had happened. Everything was circumstantial until proven otherwise. She scanned the tree line, twisted both ways when they came to a stop at the end of the road. The alley was abandoned. This area was an afterthought, overlooked and forgotten. The access it provided to a lake no one used was impassable by human standards.

Daryl brought the SUV to a stop at the end of the road, where Teri popped open the passenger door before he could offer to help again. The overhead ding an unwelcome reminder of the last time she spoke to Thomas. She hit the ground at a trot, making a line for the Camry.

Dirty windows made it difficult to see beyond the glass to an empty interior. A plastic-lidded coffee sat in the cup holder; the keys were gone. She tried the door: locked. Houses on either side of the turnaround were obscured by trees, meaning their windows couldn't see down to here either. Aside from the driver, she was alone. With only two directions to choose from, she started toward the trees.

"Sure you're all right out here?" The driver leaned out the window, eyeing her odd behavior.

"I'm fine," she said. When he didn't leave, she added,

"You can go. I brought protection." She raised the cane like a weapon for emphasis. He didn't move. If he got any ideas, the metal shaft wouldn't be much of a weapon. If she screamed, would anyone hear it? Would they come?

"That your car?" he asked.

"My friend. He'll be right back," she lied.

He frowned at her, not buying the story. The engine was running. Maybe he was concerned. Maybe.

"Have a nice day," she said, and walked toward the path. If she had to run, at least the trees would slow him down. How far was it, twenty, maybe thirty feet? The "path" was nothing more than tall weeds pushed over where someone had walked through, where *Thomas* had walked through. Once it reached the trees, even that disappeared. She made it to the curb unaccosted.

He called after.

"You run into any trouble, call me. I'll come right back, OK?"

She waved and mouthed "OK," moving deeper into the overgrowth, feeling the tension start to rise.

A few more seconds, the transmission slipped into gear, and he backed down the road, the crunch of gravel under heavy tires. He was unable to turn around with the Camry blocking the way. She watched until he was gone, took a deep breath and stepped past the tree line.

The scent of pine stuck in the air, undertones of earth and moss. Twigs crunched underfoot as she crept through underbrush. The cane made it impossible to step quietly but did an excellent job of keeping her upright while she cleared broken limbs and negotiated holes camouflaged by years of fallen leaves. The ground was dry and brittle; the air temperature plunged in the shade. Outside it was becoming a pleasant day, but in the grove she felt a chill every time a breeze worked its way through the maze of trunks and low-hanging limbs.

On the map, this area was less than an acre, nothing more than an undeveloped thicket on the east edge of the lake but as she craned to see in the confined space, it was difficult to make out more than snatches of light winking through breaks in overlapping leaves.

Straight ahead was the lake and beyond that, a smokestack visible for miles. To her left, the Shores and a strip of land just big enough to enter the compound unnoticed. Pausing in the deepest part of the thicket, she let her breathing subside, retreating until it became almost inaudible. Birds chirped nearby, somewhere outside the brush. Cars became a distant hum easily mistaken for rushing wind. Somewhere, too hard to pinpoint, waves lapped the shore.

"Thomas!"

Louder than expected, the shout broke the silence, echoed off the trees, came back amplified and distorted. It sounded hollow and weak, not quite her own. Her voice found the spaces between vertical trunks, became trapped in the dense foliage. It couldn't have traveled far.

"Thomas! It's Teri."

No answer. She hadn't expected one, but that hadn't stopped her from hoping, from wishing it could be that easy. Thorny vines and broken limbs littered the ground, making it difficult to pass, but at only a few inches high, they hid nothing. If someone else was here, a body or an injured man, she was confident it couldn't hide in this clutter. It was small solace. It meant moving forward. On with the plan.

The Lake Julian project had been a logistics nightmare from the beginning. Everyone remembered countless news articles criticizing the construction company for endless delays, unkept promises and soaring prices. The problem wasn't the community itself but the location. A coastline of uneven coves had to be straightened before any construction could begin. The lake was too shallow to support the kind of docks owners wanted and most of the ground contained chunks of hard granite. Finishing the project had been an act of will against nature itself.

Terraforming crews resolved two issues by dredging the lake, depositing the dirt they gathered as filler along the shoreline. This created more real estate and a deeper drop-off for boating and of course it cost a fortune, with investors over a barrel while developers swore the investment would pay off.

By the time they finished, what the crews left behind was a ghost of the cozy lakefront she had spent a large portion of her childhood playing in. The family park with its old metal swings and floating dock had been removed, along with all the benches and most of the massive shade trees.

She ducked low to avoid a perilous branch. Briars clung to her pants and scratched at ankles exposed where fabric shifted away from bare skin. No amount of stabbing with the blunt end of her cane pushed the tangles back enough to escape their clutches. Each one she pulled free got stomped, its brittle stalk cracked for good measure. The wilderness was a stark contrast to the manicured lawns ahead. The area had been saved from destruction only because it served a purpose.

One last gnarled, clawing growth snatched at her legs before she broke free and emerged to a brief rock-strewn shore. The sticky warmth of blood soaked into her socks, which now stuck to her ankles as well. A discomfort she attempted to ignore, greeted with the city's true motivation.

The only thing development crews hadn't been able to bend to their will was the coal plant that occupied the opposite shore. Its huge smokestack billowed white clouds of exhaust into the air twenty-four hours a day, seven days a week. At night it lit up like strands of poorly hung Christmas lights. The untamed wilderness Teri navigated to reach this shore was perfectly aligned to obscure the larger part of an industrial eyesore, which, for all it lacked in aesthetics, still provided more money to the city coffers each year than all the residents of Biltmore Shores combined. So, the economic power structure remained intact.

That was also why every lot in the development had a row of old-growth trees preserved from the original layout and several new younger ones planted in strategic places to block the view wherever possible. For those willing to become shortsighted, only the glistening lake a hundred yards offshore was visible unless they took a walk down to see for themselves.

This mattered because as she stepped out of the tangle onto the manicured lawns that abutted the lake, around the brick and wrought iron barrier, those trees were her best chance at cover. Slipping from one to another, she could cross the open spaces to her destination with ease.

Thomas wasn't lying in the brambles, unconscious or otherwise. He hadn't returned to his car, which meant he'd never left the Shores, at least not the way he'd come in. Nowhere else to go, she had to reach Roman's, try to find some clue to his disappearance. Or at the least she could find enough evidence to force an arrest and get answers another way. Even if it meant her and Roman went down together.

As Teri slipped from the shadows and darted across the first expanse of clipped grass to a wide oak, she found herself thinking about spoons. A stupid name for a theory that tried to explain the effects of chronic fatigue. She reached the tree and slid down the far side of the massive trunk, plotting her next move.

The theory used spoons as a device to represent energy, specifically the amount of energy an average person started the day with. Each activity, brushing teeth, making breakfast, driving to work, used a spoon. Teri started the day with fewer spoons than most people, and it took her longer to recover. Conserving that supply was always top priority. If that level dropped too low, which it could do without warning, she dropped where she stood. That could be running errands, climbing stairs or sneaking through yards in a private community. As it was, she felt alright, aware that might not last.

Roman's lot was the third in a single row along the straight shoreline. Going slow, she could reach it in ten minutes, maybe fifteen. That meant no interruptions or unexpected company. Over her shoulder, the first home was dark. Large picture windows with curtains drawn reflected the deep blue of the lake, the lighter blue of the morning sky and exhaust-fume clouds that lingered before dissipating into narrow wisps. It felt safe to move again.

The next spot was twenty feet at most, down a gentle slope to a large oak not far off the water. What she intended as a quick shuttle from one space to the next turned into a controlled fall as she lost her balance halfway, stumbled forward and landed in a heap on the hard ground. The dirt scraped her palms in searing red lines; her knee banged exposed rock that littered the shore. Everything exploded in alarm and pain. The fall took her breath. Clutching the throbbing bones, she contained the urge to cry out. Exposed, she had to scramble and curl herself up behind the broad trunk. She hadn't seen the root sticking out of the ground until her foot caught it. She was going too fast, getting ahead of herself. As the pain subsided, she distracted herself with a fishing boat tied to its moorings on the nearest pier. Its rhythmic thumping against the pylon was ominous, inevitable. Time marching on.

When the ache fell away, she worked her way up the trunk, careful to stay out of sight, supporting herself on the cane, reminding herself to take it slow and steady. That was two down, not bad but she needed to be more careful from here on. A twisted ankle would ruin everything..

Well-hidden, she plotted the next few moves from behind the oak tree to a large pine twenty feet away and down a slope to another point behind a large bush, not quite reaching the brick wall barrier that separated this lot from the next. The ground was even. No real trouble if she went easy. The shore was straight with two piers. This one with its fishing boat thumping against the dock, the second stretched thirty feet over the lake.

OK, deep breath.

In a sprint, legs still stinging from the fall, she made the final section past the pine to an ivy- covered brick wall with momentum to spare. Not wanting to slow down, she peeked from behind the barrier, assessed the same kind of unoccupied home as before and started across the open expanse, head low, knees bent. It was a mistake. Halfway across she froze like a baby deer. Sun glint in the corner of her eye drew attention to the patio door, where a man in his forties had just stepped out, turned and pulled it behind him. He hadn't noticed her yet, but he would as soon he turned around.

Her options were few. She was exposed, a handful of maples, a stretch of green grass and a flagstone footpath to a gazebo on the water her only camouflage. She could make it. She had to.

The gazebo was close. It took only seconds to reach its cover, dart between wood paneled benches and out the other side. Seconds that felt like moments stuck in time. No way she hadn't be seen but as she ducked into an alcove off the backside of the pier obscured by diamond shaped lattice and thick wood poles, she could see her man continue as if nothing had happened. She was safe. As safe as she could be but until the man went back inside, she was trapped like a rat in a cage.

Flat on her ass was easier than kneeling, and her legs refused to crouch. Cross-legged, she could get close enough to hug the wall and use the lattice as a view port. The man saluted the morning with exaggerated stretches, a coffee mug held high in one hand. Dressed in striped pajamas, an old T-shirt and sandals, he slid a chair from under the patio table and took a seat, coffee in one hand, phone in the other. The man seemed content to stay put for the time being.

She was right. A few minutes turned into many more, the rising sun peeked over tree tops and warmed her back, loosened stiff muscles as new ones ached from sitting still. Shifting whenever possible became a constant effort to keep cramps at bay. Keeping her legs crossed, she was able to lie flat on the deck, a position that eased tension on her spine, letting warm rays land on her face and arms. It felt good, like a lizard sunning on a rock, but the threat of discovery remained as the morning stretched on. When her toes began to cramp, curling in on themselves, she knew time was short.

It was bearable at first, flexing her feet first clockwise, then counterclockwise to release the tension. Then it grew worse, muscle fibers constricting against commands from the nerves until she had to straighten them out, forcing tendons and tissue to stretch until they released, or scream.

The coffee was gone; the phone sat face down on the table, out of the man's hand for some time. Now sandaled feet up, head bowed, he might be asleep. He wasn't moving, not even going for a pee break. Soon the swelling would come; skin would grow tight, her legs strained like sausage casings. If that happened, she was done for the day. The ache, like runner's cramps from extreme dehydration, invaded her fibers. The thought of any more became unbearable. *Screw it.*

Teri eased to her feet, using the rail for balance. The man didn't move. At full height, obscured behind a pair of posts and benefiting from the angle of the lot's rear slope, she felt confident it was safe to stand on her toes, stretching her calves. Making herself skinny as possible, she pointed her feet and pushed herself as far as she could go. Excruciating pain followed by exquisite relief as the muscles resisted then surrendered. If she had been seen, it was worth it. Dropping on her soles again, she was unsteady, but the guardrail kept her up.

She had been silent except for maybe a small groan of relief but the man's head jerked to attention anyway, focused in her direction. Rigid, she tried to become part of the scenery, nothing more than the shadow off a tree branch. Body language said everything. He leaned forward, squinting, searching the shore and the lake behind her. He couldn't see. With the sun at her back, the glare was enough to blend her in, wash out the pier and lake beyond. No way he could focus looking directly into that for more than a few seconds or he'd be seeing spots. She said a silent thank-you to whoever watched over her at times like this and focused on blending in.

"Hey." The voice carried, weak but audible over the distance "Someone down there?"

He wasn't sure. It was in his voice, a lilt that felt wary of confrontation this early in the day. She held still, waited. The pole became part of her being. The pair thrust into a symbiotic relationship. He wasn't getting an answer unless he came down and got it himself.

The man shielded his eyes, stood over the table, leaned into the sun. Nowhere to go. Behind her, green algae lapped the dock. How deep was it? Could she make a run for it? Even at this distance he had the advantage. She worked through her options, finding no good answers. There was no escape.

When the man gave a cautious look over his shoulder on the way inside, she knew it was too good to be true. She felt sick, the harbinger of something worse to come. She waited alone on the dock, acrid algae invading her nostrils while hot sun burned her neck. Sweat ran a crooked trail down her back. Wind carried the man's voice from inside the house. The response, not what she expected but what she feared the most. A set of booming enthusiastic barks pierced the air. A primal instinct took control.

A full-grown wolf hound bounded through the back door, master on his heels. The man bellowed something she didn't understand, and the dog stopped short, barking quick anticipatory yaps mixed with throaty growls in her direction. The man bent over, rubbed the dog's head and looped a hand under the animal's collar. Together they started down the hill.

Straining against his owner's grasp, the dog stood on hind legs, leaping toward her hiding space, energetic snarls paired with impatient whines. Teeth bared, it looked like he was smiling, excited to meet his prey. She considered his snapping jaws and grinning teeth, took two steps back and fell into the lake.

Ch. 8

The water was shallower than expected. Her feet touched bottom, bounced off, sending her bobbing up again. The splash was quiet, almost nonexistent. Thank God the water was warm. Of course it was, with who knew what being pumped into it day and night. No time to dwell on that. Her legs worked fine in the water, better than land by far. With the man and dog barreling down the slope, she ducked under, kicked and came out again beneath the dock. There was barely enough space to breathe with her nose out of the water but it put something between her and that enormous animal. Heavy footfalls thudded on the weathered wood planks as soon as her ears unclogged. Runners overhead provided handholds to keep herself above water. She'd lost her cane somewhere in the fall. There was no time to bother with it.

Shrinkage over time had produced gaps in the boards wide enough to make out the blue of sky beyond and the cast of shadows that passed overhead. Threatening to hyperventilate, she held her breath as the man and dog blocked the light, padded paws and slapping sandals moving past her hiding place. Claws scratched against wood as the wolfhound continued to protest the restraint. He was well trained, a dog that size could drag the man for a mile if he wanted to. They reached the end of the pier and stopped. Nothing moved. Gritty water washed up her nose, stung her sinuses, burned her throat. She choked back a cough, forced the fluid from clogged nostrils. She was safe for as long as she stayed quiet. If they looked under the groaning boards there was nowhere else to go.

She blinked grit from her eyes, waiting for the pursuers to leave. Their pacing moved from one corner of the pier to the other as they surveyed the boundaries of their domain. Heavy clomps vibrated the boards between straining fingers. The dog's expectant barking had been replaced with a determined sniffing, enhanced in the hollow space, until he sounded like a great beast instead of a household pet. Boards creaked as the canine led his master around the limited space. She hoped the lake water was awful enough to mask her scent when the heat of the animal's breath brushed her fingers, fouled the air even further. His breath was worse than anything in the water, as difficult as that was.

Their shadows blocked the light, too long for comfort as they stood directly overhead. Convinced she was seconds from being discovered, she jumped when something hard thumped the deck boards. Three times it rapped the wood, then silence. Without warning, the lake to her side exploded; a shape, large and fast in the water. Panicked, backpedaling, she pictured snarling jaws and thrashing claws coming for her. Instead of teeth, a hand broke into her hiding space, groping the air, fingers outstretched. She lurched back, avoided their grasp. The hand retreated, unfulfilled. Another thump, grunting. She pushed up, filled her lungs with air and went under.

The silhouette of a man appeared, leaned over the edge, searching the darkness for an intruder. The space was too tight to fit in without getting in the water. She prayed he wouldn't. Even in clear water, it would be too dark to make her out from above. Luck, once again, was on her side. The shadowed form disappeared from the edge but remained overhead. Venturing to the surface, she listened again through waterlogged ears. The dog's breath, like rotten garbage, filled the space; he knew she was there.

The rapping came again, three taps and a pause. In the distance a splash. No need to guess what that was.

"Come on," the man said and whistled, booming footsteps back toward shore. The dog whined, resisted. Frantic exhalations between the boards. A shrill whistle followed by claws on wood. She was alone.

Afraid to move, fingers on fire with splinters off the aged boards, she waited, listened to the silence. Tendrils of hair clung to her face. Lactic acid buildup made her arms burn. Her chest hurt, heart pounding harder than she'd realized. This was such a shit idea.

She waited long enough the pair could have walked back up the flagstone path ten times. Careful to stay submerged, she darted from under the dock and into the lake beyond, kicked hard and swam as far as her lungs would carry her. When she came up, the home, the dog and the man were obscured behind a row of trees and another brick divider that meant she had made it to the third lot. Roman's house loomed large in the distance.

She let herself bob, enjoying the freedom of floating. Life would be so much easier if she could swim everywhere. It was so much easier than walking. Despite the warmth and the filth—a pervasive grit that she felt as it clung to her skin, rubbed in her creases—the water was clear. She could see to the bottom, where a layer of stones prevented plant life from taking root. A film of algae on the surface was the only sign of growth in the lake. She hadn't seen a fish or even a tadpole. Underwater, visibility was decent in every direction. Maybe luck could throw her a bone one more time. Head underwater, she scanned the lake bottom, an expanse of stony barrens. It burned her retinas, but the pain was acceptable at this point.

Already exhausted, time was short before muscle cramps came again, before drowning became a real possibility. She had to make the search quick, make a decision to move on or give up and get to land.

Swimming in circles, she came up twice for a lungful of fresh air then dropped under again. Toward shore it was shallow enough that she could move along the bottom, using her hands to propel her body through the water. Stone after identical stone passed below while she sought out anything that glimmered in the filtered light. When she found it, her eyes didn't believe what they saw. An optical illusion, until she wrapped her hand around the cold aluminum, pulled it from the silt and surfaced again. She held the discarded cane over her head like a warrior triumphant. Buoyed by success, she made her way to shore, splashing through the shallows, and flopped on the bank in lush green grass that surrounded the brick mansion above.

The back side of the three-story monster oversaw her exhausted body, big enough to swallow her apartment and the rest of the building whole. From her perspective, upside down and a million miles away, it seemed an impossible feat to climb this mountain with a treacherous castle on top. She closed her eyes, chest heaving, questioning the sanity of her decisions. *Still missing,* a voice in her head reminded.

Once upright, the journey seemed less daunting. The last lot on this side of the lake, her approach would be a direct shot up the right embankment, where a line of evergreens shaded that portion of the property. An identical set ran the other side, giving the home a regal appearance. Tall and wide like its owner, the home's facade matched its boundary with a red brick exterior, a sloping gray roof and a row of matching gables. The privacy wall that extended from property fence to garage meant no access to the front from the back or vice versa. There was no way to be seen from the road and as long as no one was home, climbing this hill would be a breeze compared to what she had already encountered. Sliding glass doors on the back of the home were exactly where she had seen them in the satellite photos. A water-logged lump in her pocket said the black canvas roll was still there.

No one sat at the patio table with four metal chairs arranged in a circle. It looked, to her, like nobody ever had. The home was quiet, every indication of vacancy but looks could be very deceiving. Cautious, she crept along the wall, hidden by heavy limbs that reached for the ground, blending with shadows cast by thick foliage. She was silent except for the squish of waterlogged shoes.

The garage, at a right angle to the barrier wall, provided the next safe zone. It was invisible to windows on the back side and provided an opportunity to catch her breath and steel fraying nerves. There had been no sign of Thomas and no reason to believe he'd made it this far. What that meant would have to wait. For now, she was on her own.

Vertical blinds were pulled across the double-wide expanse of the sliding doors. There was no way to see inside without getting closer. On the second floor, a balcony extended from the farthest window. It's twin just around the corner, extended over the garage. It looked like both doors were shut, curtains pulled.

The air was still and stagnant. The neighborhood was quiet, her own labored breathing and the distant whine of a leaf blower on another street failing to fill the void. Lake water dripped from her hair and fingertips, making dark spots on the concrete. It felt good—the air passing over wet skin cooled her—but her throat was dry and she stunk.

Standing still meant getting caught. Waiting, increased her anxiety of the unforeseen, of the unavoidable.

The leaf blower wound down, stopped. Somewhere birds chirped. Deep breath. It started up again, louder than before. She moved. Hugging the wall gave her the option to remain hidden as long as possible, stalking under eaves that jutted off the roof, tuned to the slightest sound of movement within. She eased around until, pressed against the wall, she was inches from the glass door, able to hear any sound within.

When nothing came, she craned her head to examine the lock. A standard tumbler system, like any household assembly. Now was the time for the black canvas roll pressed against her thigh. She pulled the kit from her pocket, knelt and let it unfurl on the concrete to survey the contents, tiny silver tools exposed.

Lock picking was a skill that required talent and practice. She had neither, but she had found the kit online from a supplier overseas and even managed to open a common padlock once or twice before forgetting the kit existed. Presented with a lack of options, she hoped that her limited experience would be enough.

Through gaps in the blinds, a hallway extended through to the front door. A set of stairs ran the left side of the wall, and a green light blinking in the darkness of the foyer told her the alarm was active. *Take it slow.*

Concrete dug into her still-sore knee as she crouched eye level with the lock, tension tool in hand. The tensioner held free tumblers in place while another tool "scraped" the rest, in the trick was to line up all the holes with all the right pins. She selected a thin, flat tool and inserted it in the lock.

The tools were difficult to work with wet hands. Sweat and dirt dripped in her eyes, until she wiped them with a damp sleeve, smearing more grit into them. The tool, which resembled a bent paper clip, slid in her fingers as she struggled to find the next tumbler, and the whole thing slipped out. She cursed and started again. She inserted the tools the way the videos showed, worked at an angle, kept the tension tool under pressure. The lock twitched—she dropped both pieces on the ground with a clang of metal. She worked until her fingers hurt, afraid the tool might break in the lock. She gave up.

Shit.

Time to try something else.

The barrier to the driveway was tall, too tall really. But if the garage doors were closed, climbing the wall meant she would be exposed *and* unable to gain entry. The first nosey neighbor to drive by would end her mission. On this side she had at least the benefit of secrecy. What to do with it required more thought.

One of the patio chairs, rusted and badly neglected gave her a place to sit and think it over. The lock wouldn't give, but that didn't mean the glass door was a dead end. She pulled out her phone, wet but still functioning, and typed a web search. Sites with information on how to bypass sliding doors were surprisingly abundant. More than one suggested lifting the door at an angle, which would pull it off track. Others said a screwdriver in the upper latch would do the trick. She didn't have a screwdriver. She closed the screen.

Hands pressed against the glass, careful not to push too hard, she lifted with all her strength, attempting to free the door from its track. The site claimed that if this was done properly, the interior alarm wouldn't sound. That didn't matter, because as hard as she pushed, it didn't budge. All she achieved was smudged handprints on spotless glass, which she swirled into unrecognizable shapes with her sleeve.

Something was missing. Some way in that wouldn't alert security.

Ten square feet of concrete, barren except for table and chairs, the patio offered nothing. Likewise, the back walls were blank. No breaks except for a window the right size for a bathroom. Even if it was unlocked, there was no way she could fit through that opening. In a corner by the garage, the central-air unit hummed, offering no assistance.

A row of gables in the attic and the two balconies were out of reach. Maybe climbing the privacy wall *was* the best option. Even if it was a bad one.

Again, she scanned the windows for signs of life, stepping back for a better view. Any detail could be the answer. Any weakness the way into this fortress. Taking inventory, she paused at the balcony to the left. A movement so slight it might have been nothing. A sheer curtain, so thin to be almost see-through, shifted to the side. Too little to be caused by human interference, she figured it was a draft. Eagle-eyed, she watched, not sure it wasn't a trick of the light. When it moved again, she circled closer to the house, angled for a better look.

The opposite balcony, an exact copy with a darker curtain, was motionless. When she compared the two, it was obvious something was off. This door, the one too far up to reach, was open. A gap no more than a half inch allowed air to catch the willowy fabric as it edged through the narrow seam. That was it. Point of entry established, now she needed a plan.

Too high to climb, and even if she could, there were no footholds on the wall. The overhang that ran the majority of the perimeter jutted at least ten inches, leaving no good angle for getting over. Where there wasn't overhang, the wall went straight up to the second floor. Even an experienced climber would struggle here. She was neither.

The roof was steep but not impassable. If there was a way up, it was reasonable she could make the traverse and clear the balcony railing, which would be no more than a leg over and a drop down. *If* there was a way up.

A patio chair dragged to the eave would be too short by far, but that wasn't the only way. The trick was, while her legs were unreliable, she could still do a pull-up with the best. If she could manage to get a hand on that eave, she might have a chance.

The central-air unit, at about three feet tall, was high enough to stand on and reach the low edge. It was dangerous and stupid. If she slipped and fell, Roman would be the first and probably the last to find her broken body on the concrete. Sliding onto the square unit, the eave was low enough overhead that she had to bend her body to stand up. The unit rocked, unsteady, even under her light weight. She leaned out, back arched, until both arms found enough purchase to wrap over the rough shingled ledge. Tar and gravel cut into her arms; the sharp edge of the gutter dug into her chest. Her top half hung out too far to get a comfortable position. There was no halfway—she had to step off and trust she could scramble up without slipping and crashing to the ground.

The kickoff was easy, focusing on her upper body and grip. Trusting her arms not to let go and the gutter not to break free under her struggles. Legs kicked wildly in the air, unable to find a surface to attach themselves to. Gravel slid from the roof, and fresh cuts opened down her arms and wrists, but she held. She dangled in the air, forcing herself to concentrate. One lift, that's all she needed, one good push. She hadn't anticipated the pressure on her chest that forced air form her lungs and made it impossible to take the deep breath necessary to bring herself up. She grunted, she cussed, she flailed, but nothing changed. She was stuck and if she let go, that was it. No second chances.

Panic tried to take over but she forced it down, came to a hanging rest, letting her body press against the corner. When she gathered herself, a slow rock started, her hips swinging back and forth, gaining momentum. With every sway, she slipped but squeezed tight against the gutter that creaked under her weight. It crushed her sternum, bruised her ribs, but she focused everything on swinging her body like a pendulum. On an upswing she kicked out; her leg swung wide and missed. The gutter groaned, and somewhere a bracket broke loose, clanging to the ground. Gravity began the task of dragging her from the steep surface. On the next swing she kicked again, caught her foot on metal, but it slipped, fell free. A long arc back, another slide—one more and she'd fall, uncontrolled, unable to brace herself. One more chance. She threw all her weight into a final thrust. The edge of her foot caught the metal gutter; it overshot, but she recovered, wedged a heel in the trough, toe scuffed on the shingles. It held.

Hanging off the roof, she allowed herself a second to appreciate the victory. Then, not there yet, she pulled her free leg up and lay across the shingles, panting, horizontal on the steep incline. It was precarious, but it worked. Somehow, it had worked. The adjustment to sitting took care and patience, but finally, she was in an upright position, looking at the ground below.

Not more than ten feet, it felt like an accomplishment. A mountain conquered. Her legs dangled over, kicking the air. Breathing heavily, chest sore where a deep indentation would linger for days, she leaned back and allowed the roof to support her weight for a while.

Working across the ledge was a matter of sliding without falling off. Since she didn't have to stand, she could easily lift, shift a few inches to the side and start again. As long as she ignored the damage to the back of her pants, it was smooth sailing. The ledge that crossed the patio was narrow, just large enough to sit on, no room for error, an obstacle she negotiated with surprising deftness and found herself on the other side under the second balcony. Within arm's reach, all she had to do was stand and grab the rail.

Now was the time to depend on her legs. Legs that were shaky and filled with adrenaline. Balancing on the angled ledge, reaching out for the painted white rail, proved difficult. In the end, she managed to fall forward, grasp the wood, which held even as it strained against her weight, and pull herself across the gap. That was it—she made it. Two legs over and she collapsed on the gravel-bottomed space, shocked to be this far so fast or at all.

Tiny rocks poking into her skin weren't a problem, but exposure was. From this height a wall of windows in the next lot had an unobstructed view of the Gardners' back half, including the balcony she lay sprawled on, exhausted, staring into the sky. Cotton candy clouds drifted overhead, unconcerned with the goings-on on the ground. Time to keep moving Slowing down was death and the hard part was over. She hoped.

Her trembling hand slid in the gapped door and pushed aside the flimsy curtain. The room was empty. No one to protest when she pushed it open, slipped inside and pulled it shut again behind her. She left the tiniest crack for wind to seep through. It was important to leave no trace.

Inside the room, she slipped off her shoes and socks and held them in one hand. Lake water dripped, absorbed into thick white carpet. She cringed.

This was the girl's room. Clothes in various stages of wrinkled and dirty littered the floor. The bed, unmade, served as a depository for discarded garments and tattered notebooks. A laptop plastered with stickers sat atop the pile. A demonic teddy bear stared back from the open lid. It watched as she crossed on tiptoe, avoided contact with debris as much as possible and cracked the door on the other side. She listened, confirmed silence and eased into the hall.

The rest of the house was colder than she expected. While the AC unit had served as her stepladder it had also been turning the interior of the Gardner home into an freezer. Her skin was almost dry but what moisture that remained felt like a sheet of ice forming on her skin. When she stepped under the vent, it raised hairs on her neck where it kissed bare flesh. Wall-to-wall carpet in the same cream color as the girl's room felt like a cool layer of foam beneath her sore heels.

From here, three doors were visible and a landing that lead to the stairs straight ahead. The one behind she closed with a click, inaudible even in the vacuum of the empty home. Another, to the right and also shut, bled faint light beneath the door. That door would lead to the second balcony, another bedroom. His room. The monster's lair. To the left, an office or an upstairs bathroom. These weren't her concern, not yet. What she wanted, what she needed to see waited at the bottom of those stairs.

One by one, she worked her way down, leaning on the railing for support. Now that she was inside, adrenaline subsided. Confident that she was alone, the rush that had sustained her this far ebbed away. When this was over, she could stay in bed forever, but for now there was work to be done.

At the bottom, her first instinct was to stare down the domed camera mount that monitored the hall and foyer. Its mechanical eye focused on the spot where she stood, the same one where the woman had first appeared. The glass was dark, no operating lights. Was he watching now? She flipped off the camera and its twin in the dining room for good measure.

Time was short. No time for introductions as she set her shoes by the stairs and hobbled down the hall to the patio door. With a flick she released the catch and slid a wood slat out of the runner. Even if she'd managed the lock, the door would never have budged with that stopper wedged in there. Outside, her cane leaned against the table like an obedient puppy. She retrieved it, scooped up the canvas kit in her free hand and headed back inside. At once something was wrong.

The beep was distant at first, something that didn't quite register as wrong. Once she stepped inside, the warning tone echoed in the empty space, instantly recognizable. She was down the hall in a flash, thumping against the polished floors, confronting the white box on the wall where the beeping continued unfettered, a relentless countdown.

Digital numbers on the readout read forty-five, forty-four, forty-three. Louder here, urgency echoed in the ear-piercing whine. Next to the keypad was a message: *Deactivate?* She hit the button for yes. A new request: *Enter PIN.*

She knew this. Scrubbing back and forth over the last five seconds of last night's video, she had memorized the pattern Roman entered to lock the system. She prayed it was the same to unlock it. With careful motions she typed in 6990 and hit Enter.

Error.

She cussed.

Enter PIN.

The countdown continued as she tried again, focused on each number. Six-nine-nine-zero. Enter.

Error.

Thirty seconds.

That had to be right. She was sure of it. She'd watched him enter those exact numbers. What if it was different? What if she had the wrong code? *Stupid.*

She had to be somewhere else when this alarm went off. One hand on the knob, she opened the front door a crack. Every second would count. A car drove by, prompting a moment's hesitation. She narrowed the gap. Its shape passed in front of the house, continued down the street distorted behind crimson beveled glass. She had to try. What could it be? What else would he use for a PIN? Twenty seconds. Eyeing a stack of mail, fresh through the slot, she glanced at the inlay, shut the door and flicked the dead bolt.

With a steady hand, unsure how many tries this system gave before it defaulted to alarm, she entered a new number set. Six-nine-nine-*eight*. The screen went blank. Her heart hitched.

`Deactivated.`

In an instant she fell to a heap on the floor, back against the wall. That was it, energy exhausted. She went limp, but it didn't matter.

Ch. 9

It was beer that got her on her feet. For a long time she lay in the hall, legs extended, another victim somehow left behind. The victim of a killer who could come along at any time to reclaim her. But it wasn't fear that got her moving. It wasn't the arid desert her throat had become, making each breath a raspy wheeze, though it was a factor. The carrot at the end of her stick was an ice-cold beer waiting one room away behind a brushed silver door.

The twist top came off with a turn in her shirt, the first sip cool to the lips, dry hoppy aroma promising a good buzz. To no surprise, it was excellent beer. In her pocket a bottle of orange pills held the second part of her secret weapon. She palmed two, washed them down with a swig and let the cool liquid flow through tired veins. Adderall, breakfast of champions. She had about twenty minutes before they took effect. Until then, alcohol would ease the dull ache that made her want to lay on the cool tile until tomorrow.

"No choice today. Suck it up."

The surreal feeling of seeing this place for the first time refused to let up. It was different on ground level. This time she was part of the scene. A digital clock told her it was still morning. Plenty of time for the task of finding two people that had disappeared without a trace.

In the weak light of her phone, dark corners where cabinets hung over tile gave up no secrets. He had scrubbed every inch of this room until it was showroom clean. Even the trash cans were empty. New bags added in place of ones that contained DNA evidence. The trash can that stood beside the garage was void of any contents beyond a crumbled shard of paper at the very bottom. Mangled almost beyond recognition, she unfolded the detective's business card, a cell number scrawled in ink on the back. She pocketed the card, in case it proved to be useful.

The last thing this kitchen looked like was a crime scene. Nothing awful could ever happen in a space this well kept. Teri was looking for something other than usual evidence. Something no one else would be looking for.

The door to the garage clicked, swung open with the faintest creak on tight hinges. Staring into the space, she knew her fear of the room was irrational. The murder hadn't happened here, and the body that *had* been in that room had somehow disappeared from under everyone's nose. A Houdini act good enough to fool Asheville's finest.

Overheads hummed as they flickered to life. The room was vast, emphasized by two empty car spaces and a distinct lack of clutter. A space this big, ignored and left empty, felt unnatural. Where were the Christmas decorations, stacks of yearbooks, unused exercise equipment?

It smelled of mold and chemicals. A musty, neglected odor shot through with the pungent sweet of bleach and ammonia. An industrial combination that burned her nose and made her cough. Ice cold shocked her nerves when bare feet contacted the smooth slab. It was even colder here than upstairs. Ten degrees at least separated this room from the others, so that it was a meat locker by comparison. In the middle of the cavern, occupying the vacancy left by the Audi, she felt like her breath should be visible in white puffs of smoke.

Roman and his daughter lived in a sterile environment. One that had been scrubbed of the contaminating factors of emotion and sentiment. She had seen no family photos on end tables, no albums. Outside of the girl's room, there was no sign that a family lived here, that lives took place day in and day out within these walls. The house was more like a stage waiting for characters to appear. Like this cavernous space, it was cold.

The garage-mounted camera looked down on where she stood. It, too, was dark, the whole system shut down. She wanted to find the central hub before she left. He was a smart man, one that would have wiped the digital recordings like he had the counters and tile. Still, it was worth a shot. She had to believe he'd overlooked something.

Staring at the camera now, she centered herself in its frame. From here she would be in the exact space the center of the car had occupied last night and where it had stayed until he left, at best guess, this morning. By inching to the side, she placed herself in line with the wheel well. Now the camera was obscured, focused instead on the main part of the room. One more step and she stopped short. A metal clang echoed through the room, making her heart jump. She hadn't considered the narrowness of the space, focused on the ceiling, and had run sideways into the garage door. Its reverberations bounced off the concrete interior. The metal frame jittered where she ran into it, at once awake and active. It jolted her back, reexamining the distance between herself and the rumbling wall. That didn't make sense.

Where she stood now was the exact position of the Audi's rear end and the hiding place for at least one body. No, *just* one and that was enough. Thomas was alive until proven otherwise. She moved on before the thought took root. Back in the center of the space, realigned, she double-checked the measurements. Even at a conservative estimate, intentionally shorting her steps as she counted out paces, there was no room to park in this space and stand behind the vehicle with the garage doors closed. Especially for the man mountain that was Roman Gardner. Which meant they must have been open. Was that relevant? In the worst way.

She hadn't realized it before. He'd had an escape hatch to slip through, and she missed it, caught off guard by a man practiced in deception. The woman hadn't disappeared from the trunk, because she had never been in it. Not *that* one.

The clang of metal was deafening when she crossed the room and flicked a switch that opened the massive metal doors. They rumbled to life like thunder from an oncoming storm. Daylight found the opening and spread across the room, revealing it for what it was. When it came to a shuddering stop, she saw for the first time the driveway beyond and understood what had happened. It began a wave of nausea that spread quick like oil on water.

The driveway was empty, a wide expanse of poured concrete hedged in by rows of boxwoods and backed by the same redbrick barrier wall. But it hadn't been empty last night, and she kicked herself for not thinking of it sooner. The woman had arrived at the home sometime around five, most likely after work, in her *own* car. A car she would have parked in the driveway and one that obviously hadn't been there when the police arrived. One that Roman would have had to dispose of somehow, along with the still fresh body of his recent victim.

She stepped to the edge of the stone slab, unconcerned for the first time with being seen. The expanse of rock-flecked pavement was empty, unremarkable, but it had seen the truth, a truth it was keeping to itself. Even at eye level, the pockmarked pavement offered nothing in the way of clues. What was she even looking for? A drop of blood, a piece of jewelry? Easy to explain away. She turned and walked away, replaying the video in her head. The heavy doors clanged and jumbled back into place, returning the room to darkness. Back up the stairs, to the kitchen.

A car was hard to hide; even a small one would require massive effort. The gears had engaged in her head, turning faster than she could manage. Where could he have gone and when? Retrieving the beer from the counter, she sipped it and scanned the timeline from the moment of the murder to when the police arrived. Best guess, the murder occurred at five. According to the time stamp, the cops left by nine forty-five. Even allowing time to prepare dinner and spend the evening with his daughter, there was still an hour and a half that Roman Gardner was absent from the feed, unaccounted for. Anytime in that span he could have dumped the vehicle and the body without raising suspicion.

Lost in thought, she stepped back, caught by a stool. She settled in before she realized what it was and jumped up again. Sharing a space where the monster had sat, sizing up his victim was somehow worse than being in his home, breathing the same air. The timeline struck a chord that resonated in her bones, a wrongness that wouldn't shake. Out of the kitchen, through the dining room and across the main hall, she considered the implications. Movement might help, as if she could outrun the complication that chased her from room to room: the girl knew, and somehow, realizing that his child was involved sparked an instinct so deep in her, it was difficult to understand why it bothered her as much as it did.

She chugged the beer, draining the bottle, and paced the front room, agitated more than she was comfortable with. Maybe the Adderall was kicking in; maybe she was having a panic attack. She sat on the edge of the table, faced the couch and considered the girl. The girl had been home before Roman could have left. She must have seen the victim's car in the driveway. Chances were, she even knew the woman or at least knew of her.

From this spot, the driveway and the street beyond were clearly visible even through curtains on a wall of windows that took up the front corner of the house. From here, there was no chance she wouldn't have noticed a car leaving. Maybe she wouldn't have seen the driver. Maybe she didn't care, but when the cops came, why not say something then?

The answer was too obvious to work around. A brick wall in the middle of the road. Roman. The girl had spent the entire investigation literally under his thumb. The man hadn't moved from her side until the police were gone, until the threat had ceased. He had exercised complete control over her and never lifted a finger. The empty spot on the sofa lit a self-righteous anger that had Teri on her feet and marching to the kitchen before she could fight it. A mixture of maternal instinct and white-hot, righteous rage, pure hate—whatever you called it— filled her veins until they might burst. She had to do something, and that something might not make sense, but it was the only choice she had.

She pulled her phone from her pocket along with the crumpled business card, thought better of it and slid the phone back in. Not making that mistake again. The Gardners had a wireless phone charging on a station just inside the room. She picked up the receiver and dialed the number scrawled in ink on the back of the card. It rang twice.

"Pastore."

She flipped the card over. It had the police department seal and "Det. Dan Pastore" on it.

Driven by anger, she hadn't thought of what to say. For once, the truth seemed best.

"I have information about the Gardner murder."

The air hung thick, his end of the line quiet, muted maybe. Then it came back: an older voice, weathered but masculine.

"OK, can I get your name?"

"Not relevant," she said. This still wasn't going to take her down if there was a choice. For now, there was and it was hers.

"Can you tell me what you saw, or what you heard?"

"I saw it. Every bit of it. That bastard murdered a woman right he—" Her voice caught. "On the floor, in the kitchen. He choked her to death. I don't know who she was. I don't know what he did with the body, but I saw him do it. I swear to that."

She heard the tears crawling up her throat, felt the burn as they welled in her eyes. She forced them back, steadied herself in the doorway.

"OK, were you in the home when this happened?"

He was undisturbed by her accusation. The emotion that tinted his voice was that reserved for a child, and even that was limited. It was soothing even its direct approach.

"No."

"How did you witness the event?"

"Not important," she said.

He sighed.

"I'm afraid it is. Can you tell me what you were doing when you saw the crime take place?"

"I was watching. I know what I saw. You need to look again."

"We already checked that scene."

"I know, but he's good. Too good. Look again. There has to be something you didn't see."

His tone changed.

"Listen, I appreciate the call, but if you can't give me something solid, my hands are tied. Tell me something I can use."

He wasn't wrong and she knew it, but he asked too much. *Not yet.*

"Come down to the sta—"

"No, thanks."

"Then I can't help. You have to work with us."

She walked to the window, looked over the empty driveway.

"The car is missing."

"The victim's?"

"Yes, she drove here. She didn't drive home. Where's the car?"

"Give me a description, what's it look like?"

"I don't know."

"You didn't see it?"

"No."

"Maybe she walked. Maybe she was a neighbor. How can you be sure there was a car?"

He was doing his job, asking logical questions, but it was irritating. She hadn't asked the same ones on her own.

"Tail Lights."

"Go on."

"When he loaded her in the car, I saw her taillights."

"You saw him put the body in the car?"

"Yes." It was a lie, but a small one.

"Miss …"

"Anonymous Informant."

"Miss Informant, that's good information, but it's already in the police report. Can you give me something specific?"

"You left your card, right?"

"I did."

"Why?"

"In case something came up that was helpful. Is this Hayley?"

"No."

Now she knew the girl's name. That somehow made it worse.

"She's in danger."

"Unless you've got something I can go on, Hayley is in the safest possible place right now. Let's talk about you."

"You always this difficult?"

"Most of the time. It's my job and I'm proud of how good I am at it. Why don't you come to the station, give a statement? It's the most productive thing you can do if you want to help us solve this."

"No thanks."

"I can meet you somewhere, name the place."

"What about Thomas?"

She hadn't intended to ask that question yet, but it slipped out, needed an answer.

"Who?"

"He's the one who called you. He told you where to look, right?"

At once she wasn't so sure. It had to be him that called, it had to.

A brief pause.

"He's fine."

"Where is he?"

The man's tone shifted again—this time she couldn't pin it down.

"He's safe. Let's talk about you. What you saw."

This was going nowhere. She eyed the glass dome overhead, the source of all her problems.

"Why didn't you check the cameras?"

"Need a warrant for that. Listen, can I give you some free advice?"

"Shoot," she said.

"Leave where you are. If you're right and this man is a killer, he's dangerous. If you're reckless enough to try and fight him on your own, you're the one in danger and there's nothing I can do to help you."

"I'm not—"

"Besides tainting evidence. Anything you find wouldn't be admissible, understand?"

She nodded, knowing it couldn't be seen.

"You want to meet with me and talk about this?"

She didn't answer. Her chest was thumping again. Eyes darting to every window. Would he send someone? Alert security?

"You have my number if you change your mind. Hang up and get somewhere safe, now."

She hit the button before he finished speaking. This was a terrible idea. She was absolutely full of those somehow. What had she expected? Of course they wouldn't help—they needed evidence, evidence that didn't exist. She dropped the phone in its charger and made a run for the door. Halfway she stopped, turned and went back to the counter. Reasoning had nothing to do with what she did next; it was nothing more than pure defiance of being outdone by a system she couldn't control. Maybe the evidence wasn't here, but she knew and that was enough.

A Post-it pad stuck to the fridge had a small marker on a magnet by its side. Ripping off a page, she scrawled two words and stuck it on the marble next to the empty bottle. As she scurried from the home, using the front door this time, hauling ass across the front lawn at her quickest pace, a yellow note waited for Roman's return. Her silent statement.

"I know."

Three houses down and moving fast, her phone buzzed. It was Thomas. She answered.

"Where the fuck have you been?"

"Long story." He didn't sound right, voice subdued and tired.

"Are you home?" he asked.

"No, the Shores. Why?"

"You went to his house?" The alarm was instant.

"Just left. Headed out."

"Meet me at the gate."

"You're here?"

"Be there in five minutes."

He hung up.

Ch. 10

"You look like shit." She dropped in the passenger seat and pulled the belt across. The cane and the pick set lay across her lap. He ignored them.

Pulled into the turnaround in front of the guard shack, he had honked when she walked up, flicked the door locks. He nodded when she got in, but his eyes never left the outhouse-sized building with its closed door and tinted windows obscuring the uniformed man inside. His eyes looked puffy, darker than usual.

"Have you slept?"

"Not really. Are you OK?"

She wasn't, but it wouldn't help to go into it.

"I'm fine. Tell me what happened."

He dropped the car in gear and swung out of the drive. Tires chirped when he took the inside lane and pulled into traffic without looking. A second later he shifted to the middle, speedometer climbing, putting distance between them and the reinforced community with urgency.

She was uneasy and about more than the flicking white lines that had blurred into one. Showing anger wasn't in his DNA.

"You want to tell me what's up and maybe think about the speed limit?"

She gripped the door handle as they hit an on-ramp and raced up the incline. He eased off the gas when they joined traffic, but clenched fists still gripped the wheel.

"I'm all right," he said. "Just a little pissed off."

He was working his jaw. An uncharacteristic action that meant something had gotten deep under his skin. It wasn't clear if she should ask yet, but she needed to hear the answers.

"I'm glad you're alright. Can I ask where you were last night? Did something happen? I called you ... a hundred times."

His fingers flexed, a glance in her direction.

"Sorry," he said and his posture dropped, just a bit.

He was coming down, a ragged breath carrying waves of anger away to the ether. His face was drawn. He looked worn, defeated under the bravado.

"Thomas?"

"I was in jail." He spit the words onto the dashboard. The statement didn't make sense, but she should have guessed.

"For trespassing, they can't arrest you for trespassing. That's like ... a misdemeanor at best."

"Not that," he said.

"Then what the hell did you do?"

He shot her a look that said she should know better and refocused on the road.

"No."

"Then what else?" he said.

"That's fucking bullshit. They can't just."

"They can. They did. I don't want to talk about it."

"Thomas, you—"

"Ever," he said.

She shut her mouth. Outside, trees had thinned as urban sprawl once again peeked through the foliage, the city opening up before them.

"I'm sorry," she said. "I shouldn't have asked you to."

"You didn't. I knew better. It's my fault."

His expression said that he meant it. He really blamed himself for being locked up overnight.

"You can't blame yourself ..."

"Drop it, please."

Nothing else to say, she let it go. When the silence lingered too long, he reached for the radio, turned it low.

As they took the exit for downtown, the driver-side window cracked, paused, lowered more.

"You smell like a sewer," he said.

She recoiled.

"Thanks?"

It was true, she knew it was. The dried filth of the lake baking on warm skin made her want to puke and then shower for a week.

"You jump in the lake?"

"As a matter of fact," she said.

They turned onto the surface streets, part of the afternoon rush.

"Stupid question. Why did you jump in the lake?"

It really seemed a long time ago.

"There was a dog. I ran out of options."

"Wolf hound?" His eyebrow cocked her direction.

"Yeah. How'd you guess?"

"He was kind of cool."

She scowled, focused on the taillights ahead.

"Was he chasing you?"

"No."

"He's not cool when he's chasing you."

"Guess not. Sorry."

Traffic came to a crawl, and they sat under a red light watching walkers pass by. People she didn't know. Who they really were.

"Did you come looking for me?"

"Why else would I go there? After the cops left and I couldn't get you on the phone, I thought something terrible happened. It did, just not what I expected."

"The cops came?"

The light changed and they rolled through downtown, no clear destination.

"Yeah, didn't you call them? I thought you told them where to look."

"I told them. I told them everything about the woman and where to find her, but I didn't think they believed me. They just said 'We'll look into it.'"

"They sent a CSI team. The whole thing."

"All they told me was I had been combative, resisted arrest. I didn't get out until an hour ago."

She curled her nose—that didn't make any sense. Pastore had said he was fine, safe. This didn't sound like either.

"Where are we going?" she said.

"I don't know. I'm starving, but I feel like I need to lay down. Can I drop you off?"

"There's burritos in the freezer. You can crash at my place."

"That's alright, I need to get my head straight."

"You look like you're about to fall over. It's not safe to drive. Get something to eat, sleep it off. You can go home when you feel up to it."

No sense arguing, she wasn't backing down. He knew that. The lack of rebuttal meant she had won. They pulled off the main street and took a spot in front of the industrial brick structure that felt like a cave she had left months before. Her aching bones yearned for hibernation.

"What did CSI find?"

"Nothing," she said.

He killed the engine.

"Nothing?"

"Not a damn thing."

The answer registered, bounced around a moment before a fist hit the steering wheel. A momentary outburst.

"Bullshit."

"Exactly."

They rode up together. Thomas kept a hand on her back to push her along. The Adderall kept her nerves awake, but the muscles were finished; they threatened to fold like a lawn chair with each step. When she let them in, he lingered in the doorway, chronically uncomfortable.

The office chair caught her body as she collapsed. It molded to her contours in an overdue embrace.

"Sit down," she said.

She knocked off both shoes, freeing feet that felt swollen and smelled like death.

"Sorry about that."

He shut the door, waved a nonchalant hand. No big deal.

"Oh, hey."

He tossed her a ziplock bag.

"Good thing they didn't check the car."

She caught the still full package. The same package she had given him weeks ago. Untouched, it appeared.

"You're amazing," she said, taking a whiff of the crumbled green leaves. It smelled like sweet blueberries.

"Want some?" Her hand was already on the pipe.

"I'm alright. Thanks." He moved to the kitchen while she pulled a drag for herself, keeping some in the bowl to share later.

"There's food in the fridge," she said, coughed and spit out a cloud of smoke.

"It's not much, but you're welcome to anything. Help yourself."

"Thanks," he said, and retrieved a glass from the cabinet.

"I'm gonna try to sleep."

"Suit yourself."

She swiveled the chair around and faced the keyboard. A few taps and the screen came to life in a brilliant white glow.

"Thought you were tired."

A cough gripped her chest, ripped a spasm from lungs that burned with lake water. The burn traveled up her throat and into her sinuses. Asthmatic ejections filled the air until a glass of water appeared on the desk.

"Try this."

The water helped, pushing back another fit.

"I am," she managed. "But there's something I want to figure out."

Her body was tired beyond repair, but back in her element, where she had some control, her mind had questions. Questions that demanded answers. Even the cops were acting strange, and that meant she had missed something.

He lifted the pipe, sniffed it and took a hit, the crackle and pop like twigs in a fire, exhaled and set it aside.

"Like what?"

"Like who this woman was. Where did she come from? You can't just ... disappear."

He leaned in close, examined her eyes, studied her face. He traced lines she knew were too deep and contours now puffy.

"You need rest."

"First this, then rest. Promise."

The concern lifted her spirits. It remained clear in his features, but he frowned, and then retreated.

"OK, where do we look?"

"I don't know, but I've got an idea."

She pushed under the desk, bare feet curled in the chair. People couldn't disappear. No one was isolated. Whoever this woman was, she had been real. A flesh and blood human being. Which meant attachments. Coworkers, friends, family. Someone knew she was missing. There was a hole in the world somewhere and they could find it. If they were lucky, even use it as a trap.

"So where do you meet a beautiful young woman with a thing for manipulative psychopaths?" she said

"Are you asking?"

She turned to face him.

"No. My guess is they worked together or came in contact professionally somehow."

She pulled up the law firm website. When the image loaded, his interest was piqued. She hadn't had a chance to tell him this part yet.

"You're kidding."

"Nope." She turned the monitor for him to see. "It gets better."

"I don't see how."

She loaded the news articles and slid to the side so he could read. As he worked his way down the page, she saw the understanding seep in, the hopelessness that followed, when he reached the part about Roman going for judgeship. The man was connected.

"Well, shit."

"So, let's start with what we know."

On the firm's page a row of links led to their dedicated social media page. She clicked that. The top was a banner with the firm logo and a series of posts that featured one or all of the partners posing with local politicians and what she guessed were clients. Post after post scrolled by. She wanted something specific.

"Dead end," she announced, and closed it.

The next link was an Instagram account in the same style.

"Why would a law firm need an Insta account?" he asked.

"Massive egos and complete lack of understanding when it comes to modern culture. I don't know, maybe they post vacation photos."

The pictures were identical to the last page. A lazy social manager duplicating everything on all their channels, maybe an underpaid secretary who'd put "IT proficient" on her résumé. The images scrolled past, a series of scenes from events and galas that kept the local ecosystem running. The men appeared in most of them, Roman in fewer than she would have thought. Old women in pants suits, old men in striped suits, decrepit city officials … she stopped. Her hand had clicked before she registered the image, forcing her to scroll back up. It wasn't there. She panicked, sorting back through the last dozen entries in the timeline, until a group shot came into view.

Three men, two women. No suits this time, outside. The hair was different and she wasn't wearing makeup, but the eyes were the same; the smile had just a hint of deception. It was her.

"That the woman?"

She blinked away something, cleared her throat before she could react further. Something about this woman had connected with her on a level so deep it was interfering with objective reason. No time for that. She forced away an image that would haunt her for years; the last time she'd seen this face.

"That's her."

In a group, Roman on one end, the woman in the middle with three others she didn't recognize, they all posed for the shot. She and a redhead had their arms around each other with two older men, one with graying hair, shooting perfect smiles at the camera. In matching T-shirts and shorts, they were part of a team of some sort. The logo on each shirt was too small to read. Below the image was a caption that didn't help.

#AVLRFYL #WLGLaw #RunIt

"What's that mean?" he said.

She clicked the hashtag. A screen full of runners in similar outfits, a street downtown in the early morning, middle-aged office workers and professionals. The time stamp said August. Picture after picture showed variations on the same theme. None included their woman or Roman's team. Every picture looked similar, including one of a street she recognized, crowds lining both sides as runners crossed a finish line. In the background a clipped banner hung between poles. She zoomed in to read the words, half-cropped.

"Asheville Run for Your Life."

"Ominous," Thomas said.

She scrolled back, saved a copy of the group shot and blew it up on-screen. It was her. Two months ago their victim was a vibrant, energetic woman.

"OK. So who the hell are you?" she said to the woman in the picture.

It was getting difficult to focus through burning eyes, a fact she tried to hide as she loaded the image into a search. If a copy existed anywhere else, the search engine would find it. Maybe the woman had posted one of herself or one visually similar enough to key off the face-recognition algorithm. The results came back empty, only showing the Instagram page they'd already found. Her head hit the keyboard with a thump.

"Shit."

"Hey, be careful. You'll give yourself a concussion."

"Oh no, brain damage," she said, words muffled by plastic keys.

A hand landed on her shoulder.

"Time for rest. Come on."

She lifted her head, feeling the red indentations where the letter pattern had dug into her forehead.

"Maybe we can find an entrant list. Start figuring out who ran the marathon."

"Maybe ... but after you sleep. Come on."

She resisted, but it was useless. Her face hurt and not just from the impact. It was time to shut the system down for a while.

Her head swam when Thomas helped her out of the chair. The room tilting to a bizarre angle.

"You alright?"

"Yeah, head rush. I'm fine."

She let him guide her to the bedroom, where she stumbled straight forward, found the edge of the bed and fell face-first into the mattress. It would have hurt if she wasn't half-unconscious before hitting the covers.

"Comfortable?" he asked from the doorway.

A thumbs-up overhead, and she let the exhaustion pull her into darkness.

Somewhere in a world far away she heard him settle onto the couch. Heavy sighs and creaking of old wood. He knew where the blankets in the closet were, an old pillow that was still comfortable. She thought of them as his things, since he was the only person she trusted to stay overnight. She felt safe knowing he was in the next room.

"I'll be up in a few hours," she said, not sure the words ever left her lips.

If he answered, she didn't hear it. She wanted to thank him for taking care of her, to ask him why, but that was a problem for another time. Long awaited sleep overtook her tired brain.

It was more than a few hours before her consciousness returned, flowing in on a sea of forgotten dreams. It was dark, the apartment quiet. There were no sounds from the street. At some point she had removed the rank pants and crawled under the covers. Now she was cold. Her legs were stiff, but the ache had abated some, enough.

"Thomas?"

No answer.

She whistled, turned her head to make herself louder.

"Hey, hot stuff, you still out there?"

Silence.

Satisfied, she crawled out of bed, braced herself on the nightstand and went to the window. It would take a while to get her bearings. A cup of coffee would go a long way toward clearing out the cobwebs.

The sky was light blue but not a sunset shade. Dawn was just starting in the distance. The streetlights were still on, casting their electric haze on downtown. She had slept all night.

"Huh."

On the bathroom floor she found a pair of mostly clean pajama pants and slipped them on. Hair poking up in several places refused to be tamed by half-hearted attempts to pat it down. It was a mess that would have to wait.

As expected, the living room was empty when she poked her head out. A pillow and folded blanket placed on the center couch cushion told her she was alone. She smirked. Gripped by a dizzy spell, she grasped the door for support, focused on a spot in the kitchen and aimed that direction.

First, coffee.

Too early for the timer, she flipped on the pot and waited for it to brew. Warm earthy tones filled the air. The bubbles of percolation the only sound in the early morning silence. Drifting eyelids, lulled by the perfect peace of life before other people joined in, had her listing on the edge of sleep. Gurgles signaled completion and brought her back to the moment.

The building was waking up. Footsteps in the stairwell echoed down the hall. Somewhere a door opened, closed again.

She grabbed a mug from the cabinet, filled it with fresh brew and more creamer than recommended and hovered over the hot liquid, let the vapors fill her senses, waiting for it to cool enough to touch her lips. In between rooms, she considered her monitor, dark, and her plans for the day. When the door exploded, she screamed.

Ch. 11

The frame shattered, splinters of wood ejected inward. The door had burst open, slammed into the wall and swung back on momentum, where a thick arm was there to meet it. A large man entered. Jeans and a T-shirt, calm. The entrance, intended to stun, did its job. The only escape path blocked, she shivered, slack-jawed as fresh coffee splashed on tile. Unsteady legs retreated on their own, halted by hard counter a few inches behind. Nowhere to run.

The man assessed the room in an instant, spotted her cowering by the counter and turned so they were facing. Now she noticed the gun on his right hip. Somewhere in her brain, his face sparked recognition, but pathways too jumbled with flight reflex struggled to make the connection. Pressed hard against the counter, she had no room left to retreat. Her eyes landed on the knife drawer, too far away. Beyond him, between the intruder and the door, was a gap, maybe large enough to duck under. If she was quick, could she make it? Could she scream? His body language convinced her he could read her thoughts. A rigid finger put the plan to rest.

"Don't move and shut up."

A palm landed at his hip, fingers draped over a black holster. The safety latch was open.

"Theresa Fletcher?"

She focused instead on not losing bladder control in front of this man. The words didn't register. Too many thoughts, too many reflexes fighting for control. He snapped his fingers.

"Hey, that's you, right?"

She nodded.

He pulled the gun, leveled it, fired. The tower under her desk exploded in a shower of sparks and smoke. Her ears rang, a shrill whine that wouldn't cease. He waited while she regained hearing. Her leg was warm.

"I came to deliver a message."

He laid the gun on the computer desk and placed both hands on the monitor. With an upward jerk he dislodged the cables and launched the monitor across the room. It hit the wall next to the window. A shower of components rained to the floor.

"You getting the message?"

She didn't respond. Her brain shut down. Nothing made sense. He reached for the gun.

"Yes. I got it," she said, and snapped to attention.

"Good."

The cup somehow still in her hand trembled. She covered it with the other to make it stop. Her eyes never left his. Back rigid, she told herself it would be OK. Lied to keep control.

"You need a chair?" he asked. The concern wasn't genuine and sounded sinister in his voice.

She shook her head.

"Suit yourself."

He watched her, eyes roaming her trembling figure.

"Say something."

She licked her lips. Swallowed.

"Fuck you," she said.

"That'll work." It made him smile. "Let's get down to business."

Her chest squeezed like she was having a heart attack. If she collapsed, went into arrest right here, what would he do? Call an ambulance, watch her die, rape her dead body? All three seemed possible.

He wanted her to try something, she could tell. He needed an excuse or maybe just wanted one. She wondered if he'd kill her, wondered how. Would it hurt, for how long? She flinched when he reached for his pocket. It made him smile more, the wicked grin of a child that enjoys hurting others.

"Someone wants to talk to you."

He dialed a number, waited for the other end. When it picked up, he looked her dead in the eyes. The face clicked.

"Hey, she's here." A pause. "All right."

He set the phone on the desk, face up, dead air on the line.

"Go ahead," he said.

The voice on the speaker needed no introduction. It was a one she had never heard but knew on first contact.

"Mrs. Fletcher. How are we today?"

A million different responses, some logical, others full of hate and bile, collided, locked in her throat. No sound escaped while he waited for her.

"Mark."

The man in her kitchen jerked.

"Yeah, boss."

"Make her talk."

Mark lifted the gun, pointed it at her head.

"He wants you to talk. So start talkin'."

Mark was the first name, which meant Wallace was the last. Out of uniform he looked like a bigger asshole than the one who'd responded her to 911 call. Or maybe that was the gun talking.

"I'm having a pretty shitty day, thanks for asking," she said.

"Wonderful. That's going around. You already know why we're having this meeting, so I'll skip the introductions. The result is, I have a problem and it's you. I don't like problems. They get in my way. *You* are in my way."

Her eyes darted between the phone and the barrel pointed at her face. She leaned to the left; it followed. She shifted right; the black barrel stayed on target.

"So you can understand I have to put an end to this as quick as possible," Roman continued.

More silence. Maybe he expected her to talk. She spoke up before Mark could make a decision.

"What do you want?"

"Tell me everyone you've shared this with."

She frowned.

"What?"

"Who knows what you saw, your mother, your neighbors, the man that brought you to my house yesterday? Tell me."

"No one," she said. "Just me."

"If you lie, this will be a very short conversation."

Mark slipped the safety off, a metallic click.

"I didn't tell anyone!" she shouted. She backed away, working sideways down the counter. The gun never wavered. He was a robot waiting for an order. One that would find a way to enjoy his duties.

"One more chance. That friend of yours, Thomas Jackson. He seems to *think* he knows a lot. We'll find out how much. Now, tell me, who else?"

She crumbled, slipped, caught the ledge for support. There was nowhere to go that could escape the hollow black eye staring her down.

"I called the, uh … 911. I called them first."

Mark smiled.

"Yes, I'm aware. Who else?" Roman said.

"That's it, I swear. No one, no one else."

"Mark?"

She turned away, expecting the blast. Would she hear the shot? It didn't come.

"She's telling the truth."

"Bad news for Mr. Jackson," Roman said.

"Good for us.' He continued "Now, the bonus round. If you have any recordings, screenshots, anything you want to turn over. You may be bargaining for your life, so think hard. I'll wait."

She opened her eyes, looked to the smoldering computer, the busted monitor. A tangle of equipment and parts on the floor. She wondered how smart Officer Wallace was and bet on not very.

"It's destroyed," he said, proving her point.

"Is that all?" Roman asked.

There was no use fighting it. She looked up, acknowledged the weapon that held her captive, accepted her fate. She eased forward so only a few feet separated them. This was very *very* stupid.

"Yes. That was everything." She shivered, but her voice held firm, under strict orders. She twitched. Trails of energy like a live wire touching metal shot through her nervous system. They urged her to run, to escape, now. *Right now.*

She did nothing, waited. Faced the man and his intentions head-on.

"I believe her," Mark said.

"Good," came the response.

"Take care of her." The line went dead.

The shrug said "What can you do?" As if killing her were an unfortunate side effect. Out of his control. The second the barrel tilted, off center for a millisecond, she lunged. Hot coffee hit him in the eyes an instant before she collided headfirst with his chest. The momentum carried them both over the desk, and he landed hard on top of her on the other side. Their weight upended the chair, which came down at an angle on top of them both. She reached for anything, found the mug, clutched it in her fist and swung. It connected with his temple, shattered in her hand. His blood or hers, didn't matter. He thrashed hard, kicked her in the ribs. Scrambling to escape, she was on her feet, searching for traction when a hand grasped her ankle and yanked her down. Face-first on the floor, her head rocked, threatened to black out. She fought to stay awake.

Curled fingers clawed toward the door, his hand like a vise on her. He moved up, grabbed her leg, her thigh. Sharp nails dug into her back as she screamed for help.

In a flash he had her shoulders, flipped her over and pinned her to the floor. Veins in his forehead popped as he leaned over her body.

"You're gonna pay for that, you little bitch."

Her arms flung loose, but he grabbed them, slammed them to the floor each time she got free. She pulled loose again and he pinned her, digging a knee into her elbow. She screamed.

"Help! Somebod—" He slapped her.

"Shut up."

She screamed again.

A fist to the jaw.

"Shut the fuck up."

She whimpered, tried to scream again, choked on blood instead. She sucked in air, suffocating under his weight as he straddled her chest. She spit, a spray of red across his face and chest. Fingers clamped across her throat.

"You had to make it hard, didn't you? You're gonna die like this."

He squeezed, shutting off her air supply.

"It's going to hurt a whole fucking lot."

Spittle sprayed her face when he talked. Her eyes swelled, felt like they would explode, her face filled with blood. Under his weight, her thrashing did nothing. He rode it like a cowboy on a bull, a sick grin on his face. With each spasm, he squeezed harder. When a second hand closed on her throat, anxious to finish the job, his eyes lit up with anticipation.

Her legs were free, but his weight had crushed all the air from her lungs; they jerked, unable to respond to her commands. She braced against the floor, kicked up as hard as she could. It was enough to raise him up, and free one arm, but he came down again, crushed her ribs—she felt them crack. Lightning bolts of pain radiating everywhere. Flashes of light. Her limp arm flopped on the floor like a fish. It landed on a wad of cables, grasped and jerked hard. Something heavy collided with her hip. He leaned forward, his entire body weight leveraged against her collapsing windpipe.

Too late. Blackness filtered in from the edges. Numb fingertips traced hard plastic, sought an edge, smooth plastic, nothing to hold on to. Then they found it.

A knee, hard to his the back took all the strength she had left. The grip loosened enough that she bucked her hips and twisted. He held on. No good.

When they came down again, he corralled her legs, sat across her thighs to pin them down. It was all she needed. Arms free, she reached across her body, grasped the remnants of the shattered monitor and swung with all she had left. Hard plastic collided with skull. Glass and shards of red scattered from the impact. Mark Wallace fell in a heap to the side, hands clutched to his head. He wasn't moving.

Her heel found his ribs, jabbed into them again and again until she had pushed herself free. Stars and black clouds dotted her vision. The damage was already done, she might still die here today. She gasped on the floor, throat still closed, the panic threatening to choke off her meager air supply. Life took an eternity to return. When she could roll over, she kicked him again in the head and shoulders with no reaction. On hands and knees, she tried to scream, a rasp that ended in a bloody cough.

The door hung open on its hinges, the hall empty. No one in sight. Trembling arms struggled to support her weight, but a voice in her head said to go and go now. The desk helped her to her feet, where she hovered over the man's body like a prizefighter: listless, threatening to collapse, the monitor in pieces at his side. Using the desk for support, she picked up the remnants, held them over his head, struggling to maintain balance, and brought them down again on the back of the man's skull, taking herself down with it.

She crashed sideways into the desk drawer, bounced off and landed on her back, where she lay panting, curled up and spent, for a long time. It wasn't long before her survival instinct kicked in. *You gotta go.*

Dragging herself to the bedroom was a monumental task. Getting upright again even more so. After dragging herself up the mattress, she sat for a moment, staring at nothing. *You killed a cop,* It was still too big to comprehend. Focused on surviving this moment, she snatched the phone from its charger and hobbled back to the living room. His motionless body, crooked cop or not, meant anything could happen now. Too many variables to predict. The only thing clear was she had to leave. To put distance between herself and this. She didn't know if it was true that she had killed him, but somewhere deep inside she hoped it was.

With what she could carry—keys, her cellphone—she grabbed her cane and worked down the hall. The taste of blood was fresh in her mouth.

Ch. 12

rrational fear said he would appear any second, grab her from behind, finish the job, but as she worked down the stairs two at a time, the only sound in the building was her thump, slide, thump echoing through the cavernous space. The heavy metal door at the top, with its postage stamp window remained closed. No ominous shadows on the other side. Distracted, she felt her foot slip, slide off the step, sending her down two more on her ass.

She cried out, cursed and recovered.

The elevator was an option if he wanted to cut her off, but it made a god-awful racket that could wake the dead. There was only footsteps on linoleum when she reached the bottom, cracked the door, stepped out. The lobby was empty. Six apartments in this building, every one silent as a grave. She stumbled through the space and emerged into frigid morning air.

In the chill of the morning, she realized her skin was wet, soaked with sweat. Her thin shirt not nearly adequate in early autumn wind. Winter was far off but it had sent a messenger. Arms crossed against herself, she passed the unmarked cruiser. It occupied the space that would be hers, light bar visible through tinted glass. The street was empty, no backup. The thought occurred to take the car, to speed away as fast as possible to anywhere but here. The fact the keys were somewhere upstairs, under his body, only one of too many holes in that plan. She scurried by and crossed the street. When she hit the opposite sidewalk, she jogged, almost ran to the end of the block.

It felt like she was running in mud, depleted, empty. Like a nightmare where something chased her, but the ground refused to move. She kept going, turning every few steps to check for followers. There were none. At the end of each block, she picked a new direction and hurried down the sidewalk. Far enough along that she was almost lost herself, she allowed herself to slow, something close to a normal pace.

Her phone was charged, thank God. Fingers worked at full speed. He had to be home; it was still early. The sky had lightened to a pretty shade of blue and gold, greeting the first commuters with the illusion of pleasantries ahead. For them, the day was just beginning. She shivered again, pretending it was the temperature and not an overdose of adrenaline. Exhaustion wasn't far behind—this was too much after the exertion of yesterday. There weren't any spoons left. No answer on his phone, she pressed send on a text.

Teri: Wake up. Get out of your house, now.

She slipped the phone in her pocket.

Her chin quivered and her bones shook. Right now safety was other people, lots of them. She could blend in and disappear. A coffee shop a block away fit the bill. She could make it pretty quick even as her nerves did their dance of denial, making muscles spasm with each step. Jaw set, she continued forward, destination already in sight.

At the corner the light was red. Every car that passed suspicious, every jogger someone coming to take her down, throw her in handcuffs or worse. Head ducked to her chest, eyes closed, her arms wrapped tight to keep her warm. Pajamas and a T-shirt made inadequate morning wear. At least she had a bra on. When she looked up, a red LED hand held her in place, refused passage.

Her heart stopped when a cruiser pulled up to the intersection. Instinct said run, logic said walk away quick and inconspicuous, but there was nowhere to go. Nowhere safe in any direction. Frozen, she risked a glance at the driver, expecting to see a busted nose and a gaping wound.

The driver was normal. Another uniform on patrol. A city cop. He made eye contact, noted her clothing, or lack of, seemed to lose interest and looked away. The light changed. Clumps of people crossed from both directions, filling the intersection. She remained on the edge of the sidewalk, forcing crossers to walk around. A few glares, a "Move it, chick," but she didn't budge at all. When the cruiser switched gears to reverse and backed into a space on the other side of the street, her knees buckled. She lurched forward, having no choice, either move or fall. The momentum carried her across the intersection, to the other side. She tried not to look. Tried to force herself to keep eyes forward, to blend in, but at the last second, she risked it. The driver, who caught her eye for a second time, nodded. She jerked away and bolted to the glass door, yanked it open and ducked inside.

Inside it was warm, the chill that chased her into the packed space dissipating in the climate-controlled atmosphere. No one noticed her enter. Spaced inches apart, they waited in a zigzag line, most on phones. Bean grinders whirred, sending a nutty aroma with undertones of fresh soil into the air. The air was saturated with the banter of customers, the hiss of espresso machines and the enticing scent of fresh-brewed coffee. It made her stomach growl with each new whiff.

No chairs were available, but a worn leather couch had a single space between a man with a lumberjack beard and a girl in a college sweater with a knit scarf pulled over her face.

The girl watched her approach and offered the space; the beard scooted without taking his eyes off his phone. She accepted with the best smile she could muster and tried to disappear into the sinking leather. This was better—at least there were witnesses, and somehow that felt important—but she still stuck out. She needed clothes, food and a plan, but first she opened her messages.

```
Thomas: What's up?
Teri: We're in deep shit. You need to meet me.
I'll explain when you get here.
```

She hit Send, typed out a new message.

```
Teri: Don't go home.
```

Send again.

A second later the phone rang.

"Yeah."

"What happened?" Her stomach clenched at the thought of explaining her morning so far.

She gave the beard a sideways glance, turned to the side. Phone nestled in her shoulder, she hissed into the receiver.

"A cop broke in. He tried to kill me." No one cared—no one was listening—but it felt wrong to say the words out loud.

"I don't understand. Like he tried to arrest you or he—"

"He shot my computer and … he wasn't moving when I left."

A shift on the couch drew her attention. Beard got up, walked out of the shop.

What had he heard?

"Where are you now?"

"K's on Patton."

"Alright, I'll be there in a minute."

"Thomas."

"Yeah."

"Roman sent him, to deliver a message. He said you were next."

"Thanks for the heads-up."

"Keep your eyes open."

She looked up as two uniformed officers walked in.

"And hurry."

She hung up.

He was there in ten minutes. When the call came, she was in a restroom stall, feet on the rim so they were hidden from the outside.

"Hey, I'm here. I don't see you."

"I'll be right out."

Slinking out of the bathroom, she grabbed him by the arm and pulled him outside. The blast of cold air was a shock to the system and she was limping now. Swelling had started in the ankle the cop had wrenched. Thomas was gaping at her but she ignored him. His car wasn't outside. It wasn't up the street in either direction.

"Where did you park?" she said.

"Around the corner."

"Let's go."

She made it around the corner, found the car sitting in the same spot the cruiser had been and lifted the handle. Locked, obviously. Hairs stood on end until Thomas caught up and let them both in. Shutting the door shut out the rest of the world. It was a start. She was safe in the car. They were safe for now but they needed to get somewhere else, fast.

"Your neck is bruised."

She flipped the visor mirror, saw herself for the first time and flipped it back. No desire to see the purple ring that had formed above her shirt collar, a line of red she hadn't noticed on her forehead or the swelling that had started over her left eye. There was enough pain everywhere else to focus on.

"Are you OK, do you need a doctor?"

"I'm fine. Let's go."

"Teri."

"It's cosmetic, I promise."

She twisted, which sent a tidal of wave agony through her entire body. She did her best to play it off, failing miserably. In the mirrors: No uniforms, no sirens. They really weren't coming.

"Can we go, please?"

He flicked on a blinker to pull out.

"Where are we going?"

She thought about it. Was anywhere safe?

"I don't know. Somewhere to think. Someplace quiet."

"On it."

She felt better as soon as they pulled into traffic. Movement of any kind eased fried nerves. Satisfied the need to run and never look back. Familiar buildings passed, sinking into the rearview.

"You want to talk about it?"

She shook her head.

"Are you hurt?"

"Yes, but not bad. I'll live."

His expression said he didn't believe her but wasn't going to press it. They took the highway ramp and headed away from downtown.

"This guy was a cop?"

She did her best to explain as they drove west, morning traffic crowded on both sides, a light frost clinging to the windshield. She told him about the phone call, Roman's even tone when he demanded information and when he handed down her death sentence. She skipped over the fight as much as possible, saying only that she hadn't seen any signs of breathing but had left quick. Maybe she missed something vital.

She swallowed hard. It hurt to breathe.

"So I'm next?" he said.

She bit down hard on her bottom lip, fighting the tears that seemed always on the verge of coming lately. Her entire life had come off the rails in a few short days.

"I'm sorry," she said.

"What the hell. What for?"

Her attention stayed focused out the window, not wanting to face him.

"I got you into this. You know too much. What if he had come to your place first, what if ..."

A short pause.

"Thank you," he said.

She sniffed, turned to him.

"Why?"

"You kicked his ass."

"I think I killed him." She found a spot in the floorboard, focused on it.

"If you hadn't, *he* would have killed *you*, and I would have been next. You saved us both. So, thank you."

She curled up in the seat, searching for a way to handle the situation. Emotions that didn't make any sense ran hot. She was coming apart at the seams.

"Don't worry about it," she said.

After a while they took another exit and the Camry headed south.

"You've been through a lot. You're shook up and you should be, but I need you to hold it together alright?'

A hand landed on her leg, a gentle squeeze.

"We'll figure it out."

She set her hand on his, nodded.

"OK."

The farther they went, the more her chest loosened, heart rate returning to normal.

"I'm sorry," she said.

"You gotta stop saying that."

"It's my fault."

He scowled at the road.

"Listen, try to understand. I'm a grown man. I make my own choices. I choose to be here with you. So, stop feeling bad about it and stop apologizing, OK? Roman is the monster here."

She nodded again.

His expression softened, taking in the broken form she must present, balled up like a child in the passenger seat.

"You look tired. I know somewhere we can go for a while."

Off the highway, they pulled into the parking lot of a new three-story hotel, mostly empty this early. Thomas pulled under the check-in awning and parked. Her eyes landed on the security camera positioned over the automatic doors with its tinted black dome, and she slid deeper into the seat.

"This OK?" he said.

She nodded, tired of talking.

"I'll be right back."

"Be quick," she croaked.

"I know this guy. Sit tight."

He jogged around the back side of the car, passed through the glass doors and disappeared inside. The heat from the blowers felt good on her skin. She turned up the thermostat and adjusted the vents, letting them do their job to ease the shivers. They only did half of it.

Twisted in the seat, she watched a dome over the door, peering through the tinted glass, unable to make out anything.

More cameras hung from the corners of the building, one facing each direction. She buried her head in the door. *Just hurry.*

He was back quick, as promised. A new blast of cold filled the car when he got in, slamming the door shut. He handed over a key card.

"Third floor, this side so we can see the parking lot," he said.

He pointed to a row of windows on the top corner.

"That one, I think."

"How did you check in?" she said.

"What do you mean?"

She shifted to sit up as they pulled from under the awning and into the parking lot. Her ribs still throbbed with each breathe and screamed if she put pressure on the wrong side but she was getting used to how to move. He chose a space close to the door.

"I mean how did you check in? What name did you use, a credit card, anything traceable?"

His face told her he hadn't thought of that.

"No, I just told the guy what we needed. Said we might be here for a few days. You're right, sorry."

"Can you trust him?"

"We're not fugitives."

"We're not? Maybe you aren't, but …" She wanted out of the car, but something told her this space was too exposed.

"Yes, I trust him."

She thought he did but could *she* trust him? A complete stranger.

It didn't matter; there was nowhere else to go. She noticed a parking spot under a tree by a side entrance.

"Park there," she said.

He didn't argue. They pulled out and moved to the new space, well hidden from the front doors, but most important, the tree blocked the security camera's view of their car. He was considering what she'd said.

"My guy's the night clerk. Doesn't care who's with me, just letting us use an empty room. They're pretty slow this time of year."

"You do this a lot?"

His eyes narrowed.

"No."

She sighed.

"I don't care. Come on."

Ch. 13

Too far from the elevators, she leaned on Thomas to limp toward their room. The ankle felt like it was still swelling and rolled whenever she put pressure on it. With each wince of pain, she saw the concern grow deeper.

"Just a sprain. Relax. I've had worse."

They made it together, taking half-hop steps until they reached the door. He let her balance on the wall while he slid the key card in, the light switching from red to green.

"You need a doctor."

"I need some sleep," she said, and edged past.

The room was large, a table with two chairs against the wall, floor-length curtains drawn and a king-sized bed. With a little help she hopped to the edge of the mattress and took a seat, relieved to be off her feet.

"Dibs on the couch," he said, motioning to a two-cushion love seat by the window. She started to argue, pushing herself back on the bed, lit up again with a fresh stab of misery down her side. Her breath caught—inhaling was absolute agony. She had a cracked rib for sure, but he would never let it be if he knew. She collapsed in a pile of active nerves on the other side.

"You sure you're OK?"

"I'm wonderful. Just need sleep," she grunted.

With her good leg, if there was such a thing, she kicked herself into position, covered her head with a pillow.

"Don't wake me up. Ever."

"About that."

One of the chairs scraped the floor. The wood creaked under his weight, the only sound in a quiet space.

"You need anything? I can go grab supplies since we're going to be staying a while."

"Like what?" she muttered.

"Like ... clothes, pills ... woman things."

She peeked out, incredulous.

"Woman things?"

"I don't know. That's why I'm asking. If you can't go home for a while, what do you need?"

He was right, but the things she needed couldn't be bought at a normal store. They were complicated, controlled.

"I don't have my sleeping pills. That's a problem. Insomnia can keep me up for days. I need clothes, I guess. Can't go out in pj's."

She cradled the pillow to her chest, padding insides that felt broken and rearranged.

"Pain pills, for the love of God. I need my stuff. I need there not to be a fucking dead cop in my apartment. I need—" Another jolt of pain in her ribs.

"Alright... relax. Something for pain, something for sleep, something to wear. Is that right?"

Nodding. "Yeah."

"Are you hungry?"

Her stomach moaned at the thought of food.

"I could eat your leg right now."

"We can do better. I'll be back soon. Try to rest. I have the key, so don't answer the door."

"Don't worry."

She listened to his muffled steps fade down the hall. Shutting out the world, retreating into a safe place somewhere deep inside, she heard the elevator, its noisy doors clanging open and then shut again. After that, nothing. Sleep didn't come, it wouldn't. She lay somewhere in between, where exhaustion claimed her body but her mind refused to rest. Nightmare images danced in the dark places behind her eyelids. Promises of things to come. Rubbing them until stars exploded from her retinas did nothing to change the scene. The demons were here to stay. She tossed the pillow.

"Fine. Coffee."

The rooms had single-serving coffee makers with pods. Using the wall for support, she hobbled to the bathroom, ran water in a paper cup and poured it in the machine. She popped in a pod, not caring what it was, and hit brew. The machine gurgled and hissed as it prepared to fill the tiny cup. All the sugar was fake and the creamer was powder, but anything was better than nothing.

At least the phone was charged, small favors. She huddled over it, scrolling through news articles, looking for anything on the missing woman. It might be her own name soon on a fugitive report. How long before someone noticed the unmarked at the curb, before they smelled the body in her apartment? The clock was running, and she had no idea when time would finally run out but at least she got to choose who went down with her.

Sitting at the table, the coffee was boiling, so she sipped it and let the liquid do what it could to soothe her aches. The warmth was pleasant and it felt good to have something in her stomach, even if it felt like she'd been punched by a prizefighter for seven rounds. It was baby aspirin for a broken leg, yet every bit of relief counted.

News was a dead end. She closed the feed and switched to Instagram. It was a mistake, but sometimes you had to poke a bruise to remember why it hurt. Scrolling to the image, she tapped it, zoomed on the woman with no life to be found. The question that seemed impossible to answer, the one that tied their fates together for better or worse.

"Who are you?"

She was beautiful. Young, of course, but alive in ways Teri hadn't felt for years. She looked energetic, motivated. As always, her smile said she knew something and it was her secret to keep. Teri set the phone on the table, brought her knees up and stared at the screen. *It could have been you.* They had come close to sharing a grave today. Would anyone come looking if she disappeared? What about Thomas? This wasn't his fight. He'd been dragged in by his own willingness to help others. He was right about one thing: if Roman got away with this, she couldn't live with herself. No one else could be his victim.

She had Maps open, studying the roads that surrounded the Shores, when the door clicked. A second later the aroma of pancakes and syrup filled the room. Thomas came in with a pair of plates turned over like covered dishes.

"Thought you were sleeping?"

"Overrated," she said. "What you got there?"

The grumble that began in her stomach seemed to consume her entire body, which already knew it wanted whatever was on that dish. The makeshift lid was off before the plate touched the table. A steaming stack of flapjacks, sausage and fluffy eggs smelled like heaven on earth.

"This is amazing."

"They have a whole buffet downstairs."

He set his own plate down, revealing a similar banquet.

"Do they have forks?"

He whipped out a set of plastic-wrapped utensils, one each, and took a seat across the table.

"It's not much."

It was, but she couldn't respond, having already attacked the plate like a starving bear. She shoved delicious morsels in her mouth as fast as they would go. How long had it been? Days … it felt like forever. The realization she was starving had taken a backseat to the other damage her body had endured, but as soon as the opportunity arrived, it came roaring back. She mangled the eggs in no time, but the pancakes gave her trouble. She had to stop and sip coffee to keep from choking on their spongy consistency. It hurt her throat to swallow that hard. She pushed the plate away, forcing herself to slow down. For the first time, she noticed he wasn't eating, just watching her with a piece of syrup-glazed sausage on his fork.

"Sorry, I'm starving."

"It's fine … I've never seen you eat like that."

"It's been a while."

He examined the plate, already half-empty.

"You want some more? I'll go back."

She shook her head, already regretting eating too fast.

"No, this is fine. Thank you. So much."

He bit the piece from his fork with a smile.

"Anytime. What are you working on?"

Her phone was on the table, pushed to the side when the meal arrived. The screen was dark.

"Looked like a map when I came in. Did you think of something?"

"I don't know … I was trying to think of something. Trying to come up with … a plan, I guess."

"Show me what you've got."

"That's it, I don't have anything."

She pulled the phone over and hit unlock. A map of Biltmore Shores, zoomed out to show the neighborhoods around Roman's, showed that there weren't many secluded places nearby.

"I figure he didn't have long to dump the body, but I can't seem to figure out where."

Thomas stood, grabbed a pen and paper from the bedside and sat back down, pushing their plates out the way.

"Alright, so let's think logically. How long did he have from the time the murder took place until the cops showed up?"

She rubbed her eyes, trying to remember the exact timeline.

"Like, three and a half hours, but he couldn't have been hiding the body because he was cleaning up the evidence."

He was writing, putting down times.

"When did he kill her?"

"About five … I think. It was pretty close."

He wrote 5 p.m.—murder.

"OK, and the kid got home around six?"

"Hayley, a little after maybe."

He noted 6 p.m.—Hayley home.

"What else?"

"They had dinner and she sat by herself for a while in the living room. That was like seven thirty, I guess."

"Where was Roman?"

"I don't know, but he changed clothes."

"So that's our window. When they finished dinner to whenever the cops came is when he got rid of the body."

In two days the woman had become "the body." How long before she was nothing? An accident that no one figured out and no one remembered.

She frowned at the timeline he had drawn out.

"What?"

"That doesn't make sense. That only gives him thirty minutes, and that includes washing up, changing clothes. Where could he have gone in that time?"

Thomas slid over the phone and examined the map.

"The lake?"

"How? There's no access big enough for a car from here, and the power plant is on the other side. Everything else is developed. You'd be seen."

Bent over the screen, he pointed out a large section of tree covered shore.

"Here?"

"No good, it's an industrial park. Look."

She scrolled back and revealed a wide white rectangle surrounded by parking spaces that stretched back from the lake. The building was big enough for several hundred employees.

"Look, there's a fence and a gatehouse. You're not getting through there unnoticed."

"OK, so not the lake."

She nodded.

"Then where?"

"I don't know. He wasn't sweating. Not more than usual, and you can't dig a hole that fast. He must have stashed her somewhere. In the woods maybe."

"Are there any places like that nearby?"

He was already panning around the satellite image.

"A few, but I don't know where to start. We'd have to cover all of them one at a time."

Thomas sat back.

"That would take a long time."

"I don't think we have time. They're going to find that body …"

He placed a hand on hers.

"Stop. don't think like that. You don't know that you killed anyone."

"I'm pretty sure I did."

"You don't *know* it. Look at you, it's amazing what people can live through. Right now, all you did was save your own life and get out of there. All right?"

"What if?"

She hugged her knees, a searing line tracing her left side.

"What if you did? He tried to kill you."

"He was a cop."

"That tried to kill you."

"I can't prove that. He deserved it and I'd do it again, but they send you to jail for this and you don't get out. Ever."

He wanted to argue, it was clear, but he thought better of it and changed strategy.

"Let's focus on this right now. Worry about what we have control over. If we can prove Roman did this, we can prove he sent that guy after you, OK?"

"If."

Saying that had been unnecessary; she tried to go on.

"Alright, but without evidence, without something concrete, we're not proving anything. This guy is connected, he's a professional and now we know he's got friends inside the sheriff's office. So, unless we find this woman, I don't know what we can do."

"So let's find her."

The pad moved again to the center of the table, a new page open.

"What do we know?"

She dropped her arms, letting her head fall with a thud on top. The impact lit up nerve endings down her spine. Flashes of red and white behind bloodshot eyes.

"Oh God, that was stupid."

"Hold on." He said

He fished a bottle from his pocket, set it on the table with a clatter of pills inside.

"They had these downstairs."

She eyed the bottle: maximum-strength pain reliever. Maximum over-the-counter strength.

"You just remembered these?"

He flushed.

"Sorry."

She picked up the bottle, popped the top like a Pez dispenser. Sighed.

"Thank you."

"Don't worry about it. Let's figure this mess out."

She took the max dosage, then doubled it. A handful of white chalky pills washed down with already cold coffee, and she was ready to try again.

"OK, so … what do we know?"

"We know Roman Gardner is a flaming asshole and a woman killer."

"OK."

She eyed the pad.

"Write it down."

"Flaming … asshole. Got it."

It earned a grin.

"We know he hid her body, but we have no idea where."

He continued taking notes, putting each item on a new line.

"Anything else?"

She shrugged.

"I don't know. Whoever this woman is, she's important, but for whatever reason, no one seems to be looking for her. That's strange, isn't it?"

"It is."

He wrote something else.

"Let's try something different. What do we need?" He asked "To get you out of this, we need a plan."

"We need a body." she said

"But we don't know who she is, so first we need to figure out who she was and what she was doing."

He wrote both new lines.

"I can check the entrants list. It'll probably be by company. It means a lot of research, but maybe we'll get lucky," she said.

"Good start. She was on his laptop, right? That's why he went off."

"Yes."

"Maybe we can find that. Figure out what she was after."

She kicked herself as soon as he said it.

"I was in the house. I should have done that."

"I doubt he leaves anything like that at home. My guess is someone this careful would keep it on him. It's probably in his office, or his car."

"We can't get to either one."

He underlined the entry.

"We'll come back to it."

He slid the list over.

"This is what we've got."

She read the list, a page full of questions without answers. A plan but no direction. She stood, picked up the list, thinking of something else they should add.

As soon as she reached her feet, blood rushed from her brain. The room went dark; she swooned and caught herself, teetered on the edge of blackout until the world she knew faded in again.

"You need to lay down."

"Agreed," she said, and let him guide her to the bed. The stabs and jolts hurt less than before. The pain pills were kicking in. If she could sit upright, they could set a course in action, but she couldn't and the thought didn't last.

Ch. 14

When she opened her eyes, he was gone. The room was quiet, still. Her face smashed against the fresh pillowcase on the overstuffed pillow. She wanted to lie there forever. The quiet embraced her, promised to heal her wounds. She shrugged the comforter over her shoulders, curled in the fetal position. Just a few more minutes before the peace ebbed away and life took its place.

Her bladder had other ideas. A tentative foot tested her weight. It hurt, a dull throbbing ache, but nothing that couldn't be managed with more pain relievers. The bottle, she noticed, was sitting on the nightstand, a slip of paper slid underneath by the key card. No time to read it, she pushed off the bed, balanced with one foot flat, toes touching on the other, like a ballerina and worked her way to the bathroom. *Hold on, I'm coming.*

Just once it would be nice to wake up and not feel like she'd been hit by a truck. Her foot caught the rug, sent her forward. She braced on the doorframe and slammed hard into her shoulder, let go and fell into the room. The toilet caught her fall, cold porcelain on skin. She turned and sat on the closed lid to catch her breath. *Just one.*

What time was it? What day was it? She stumbled through a fog of recognition. Her mouth tasted like sand and film, and she hoped there was still time to add a toothbrush to that shopping list. Regardless, the mirror was the enemy today; she ignored it with fervor. Even washing up and hopping back out the door, careful this time, she refused it the power to destroy her optimism. Things always looked worse than they really were, and she was pretty bad off, so best to skip the freak show.

The hotel was alive now. Doors opened and closed down the hall. She could hear TVs and conversation from other rooms. Still not a packed house but not the graveyard it had been before. The thump of her heart was audible, a combination of detox and exertion. She moved to the middle of the room, using the bed for support. On one foot she reminded herself of Daniel-san from *Karate Kid*. Head bowed, she listened to the activity around her, took a shallow breath, still unable to expand her chest to full capacity, and let it out slow. She repeated the process two more times. The doctors that had pushed meditation on her as a kind of pain relief were bullshit, but staying calm was the key to managing any situation, and there was plenty to manage. When she felt more at ease, she went to the bedside, sat on the edge and read the note under the pill bottle.

T,

Went out for dinner, etc.

Be back soon.

—Thomas

While she read, she rubbed her jaw, tender although still working. Hadn't noticed that earlier. Whoever watched over single disabled women had their hands full, and she thanked them for their efforts. The overseer who had made her with faulty wiring and sent her from the factory full of defects had seen fit to keep her in service a little longer, and that was something.

She reread the note. He signed his name with straight, tall letters. It was neat and direct. Neat he was, but direct, not always. Thomas had a way of holding things back, waiting for the right time. She felt like he kept a little beneath the surface, just a piece of himself no one else could see. They had been friends long enough she didn't deny him that. There was plenty she never shared, secrets even he didn't know. Nothing life altering but enough that there was space between them. One curated to keep her safe and one she had to bridge since he was keeping her alive now. A space not unlike the one opening in her belly right then that demanded more nutrients to repair her broken body.

There was a spare room key on the table, that Thomas seemed to have cleaned before leaving. Which meant it looked like time to risk a trip to the vending machines. A rubber band in the top drawer beside a Gideon Bible held her hair back, and a handful of pills would keep her numb.

Switching arms, she was able to lean on the cane and keep pressure off the injured ankle. With a halfhearted hop she could limp pretty far, just not very fast. Like an old war veteran, she struggled past the heavy door and out of the room.

The amount of pressure her ankle would take was encouraging. It was probably just a light sprain. A few days and she might be back to normal, whatever that was. On the way down the hall, she tested it, taking half steps, gripping the cane handle and stifling little yelps of pain. It wasn't ready, but it would be. She had to lean hard on the battered-rib side, holding her arm close to shift pressure away from the ribs. Still tender, they didn't scream like stabbing knives with each breath. Maybe they weren't cracked, maybe she was the luckiest girl alive. Maybe pigs could fly.

In an alcove beyond the elevators, the vending machines beckoned with an electric hum. Two for water, sodas and sports drinks and one for the foil-wrapped sugar bombs she craved more than anything. The lime green sports drink was the best choice, something to replenish fluids, electrolytes— whatever those were—but chocolate and caramel had her in its spell. Maybe both, they could balance each other out. It didn't matter, anything that would fill the pit in her stomach. She balanced on the cane, stuck a hand in her pocket and dropped her head. No purse, no wallet, no money. Perhaps the real concern should be signs of concussion. How could she forget money? Spirits dashed, she limped out of the humming, poorly lit space.

Going back to the room was too depressing, and she needed something to sate this appetite. The elevators were just behind, but their stainless doors shook when they opened and made her uneasy. Also, elevators stopped at other floors and that meant having to ride in a small space with other people. Without a shower and smelling like death. It would be hell for everyone.

A sign with a jagged line on the far end of the hall indicated a stairwell going down. She limped to it, backed into the push handle with an audible release that echoed off the cavern within and stepped inside. The door to the stairwell, hollow and industrial, sounded like cell slamming shut. In the silence that followed, every movement amplified off tile and stone. She stepped forward, steadied herself on the first step and eased down.

Down was the easiest. If she went slow, it would take longer, but she could make it. Maybe there was something sweet to get her hands on down there. A prize at the end of the maze for a very determined lab rat. The first flight, simple enough, convinced her to keep going slow and steady. By halfway down the next, the repetitive motion robbed her of speed and balance, but the muscles and tendons cooperated enough to reach the landing. She touched bottom at least ten minutes later with a slight tremor and a mild sense of victory. At times, even this small amount of control felt essential. On that high, it was easy to cross the open space and exit to the downstairs lobby.

On the other side, the room opened to a single space, rustic chic decor with leather couches for guests and a faux wood fireplace. It looked like a modern take on a country inn and accomplished neither. Behind the desk, a young woman with a tight bun and a pen sticking out was busying herself with a computer screen. A couple waited as she typed.

To the left was another hall and a sign that said POOL-GYM-SAUNA. Food sounded good, but this sounded better. Maybe there was a hot tub. That alone would make the effort worth it. Moving down the hall, she reached a large glass door with a pull handle.

The gym turned out to be a couple of stationary bikes, a stair climber and some free weights. Through the window she could see the pool was outdoors and covered with a slate gray tarp that sagged in the middle. Through another glass door she found the sauna. A tiled room with an in-ground hot tub small enough to touch both sides at once. Secluded and warm, it felt like a good place to sit for a few minutes. The steam felt good in her sinuses and she had the place to herself.

Kicking off her shoes, she let her feet dangle in the water, which was aerated like it had bath salts in it. The distorted refraction of her toes waved back and forth beneath the surface. A nasty purple ring around her leg looked faded and less alarming in the tinted pool. Head lowered, eyes closed, she considered tumbling in. The water was too shallow to drown in, but if she lay very still on the bottom, maybe no one would find her for a while. Tears came and refused to be held back this time. They fell like rain on her legs and arms, eventually rolling into the water below. Her body jerked with a sob that need to break free, and soon she shook, heavy, long moans that echoed off the tile. The proof of her own helplessness made it worse. She wrapped tired arms around her body, holding herself together in more ways than one. The pathetic voice inside wanting an end to it all. Sensibility chastising her as she bled emotion into clear water.

Go ahead, have a breakdown, that'll help everything.

The words cut deep, a wound that wanted to blossom until it consumed everything. Control was necessary, but so was release. She tried to fight the breaking dam but failed. Instead she let it come, let it wash over and through her. Every fear, every disappointment, her pure hatred and self-loathing. She let all the unacknowledged failures, the fears of further decline, everything she was afraid to admit to herself, pour out. She bawled like a child until she was empty and hollow. Until all she wanted to do was let go, slip into the pool and under the surface. To let the warmth hold her until it was all over. Then it was enough. She let the tears fall but denied them her self-pity. She stemmed the flow, focused on the glistening patterns that danced across the ceiling. With a sniff and a hard swallow, she was done. Enough weakness for one day.

A slam in the next room made her jump. She jerked to attention, swiping at puffy eyes. The outer door opened and a shirtless man came in, wearing shorts and a towel like a lion's mane on his shoulder. It blended well with a chest full of gray hair. He stopped short, seeing her for the first time. Even his arms were hairy.

"Oh, I'm sorry. I'll come back," he said, ducking to leave.

"No, it's OK."

She got to her feet, slipped back into now wet shoes.

"Go ahead."

She slipped past him and through the gym before he could argue. This time she passed the stairs, noted the abandoned lobby and empty dining room and went straight for the elevator. It was time to get back to the room and find a way out of this mess. No avoiding her reflection this time—the distorted image in the doors was twisted, inhuman and, she thought, not far from the truth. When they opened, she stepped into the car, thankful it was empty.

"Alright, you've had your cry, now woman up. Get your shit together."

The pep talk was familiar and one that she responded to well most of the time.

In the room, she crossed to the window, pulled open the curtains. The Camry was back, a black shape beneath pale yellow foliage. Ahead by only minutes, she took a seat, crossed her legs and waited. The door clicked less than five minutes later; Thomas entered with bags in hand.

"How come every time you leave, you bring me food?"

He shrugged.

"You gotta eat."

"If I eat everything you bring, I'm gonna be huge."

He slung a black backpack from his shoulder to the bed and set the white paper bag he was carrying on the table. A plastic gas station one still in hand.

"So you don't want it?"

She dug into the takeout before he could pull it back.

"Oh, I want it. What's in the other one?"

"Shopping list."

The takeout was cheeseburgers. Delicious greasy cheeseburgers with lettuce and onions. Still chewing, she pointed the wrapper, stained with ketchup and mustard, at Thomas.

"You're in charge of meals from now on."

He retrieved a second silver wrapper and tossed the bag aside.

"What have I been doing?"

She nudged the plastic sack.

"What did you get?"

It dropped on the table with a heavy thump. A slender silver and blue can rolled out.

"Check it out."

He held the drink up like a prize.

"Red Bull?"

"For energy. It's not ideal, but it'll work, right?"

"It's perfect." She popped the top, downing a quick swig.

"Jitters are my favorite." She gave a grin.

The next item was a small reddish brown bottle with a clear plastic cup on top. She took it and laughed.

"Cough syrup?"

"For the insomnia. Take a little before bed. It *might* help."

"You're unbelievable. Not doctor recommended, I'm sure, but ... screw it. Worth a shot. What else did you do?"

Watching each item he pulled from his care bag made everything seem just a little less awful, and that was unexpected but welcome.

"The best yet."

He held in his hand an orange wrapper with yellow writing that made her eyes go wide. A king-sized Reese's chocolate cup.

"You do know me."

"I do what I can."

She took the candy and set it aside.

"This is dessert. We're sharing this."

"No thanks, watching my figure." He winked.

"Screw that, you're having one. I'm not enjoying this alone."

He bowed and pulled up a chair, opening the burger wrapper in front of them.

"Hey, thank you," she said. "I couldn't do this without you."

"You could, but I'm glad to help."

She reached a hand across, a bridge between them.

"Wouldn't want to."

They ate in silence, both enjoying the delectable combo of meat and salt and fat.

"This is delicious. Thank you so much," she said again.

"No worries. Hey, I got something else."

Crossing to the bed, he pulled up the backpack and unzipped the top.

"I keep some clothes in my car for emergencies."

She raised an eyebrow as he pulled out a stack of dark athletic wear.

"It's just some track pants and a T-shirt, but they should fit if you tie the string real tight."

"Come over here, so I can hug you."

"You're welcome," he said, and set the clothes on the bed.

"Want me to put them in the bathroom, by the shower?"

She scowled, trying to hide a grin.

"What are you saying?"

"That I can smell you from here."

"I'll get them, thanks," she said.

"Just in case."

He walked the fresh clothes to the bathroom and left them for her. When he came back, he stood with hands on his hips, like a man surveying a work site. He was looking for something else to do.

"Why don't you sit down for a while?"

He rubbed his head and smiled. He looked tired, worn.

"I think I'm gonna lay down instead. You need anything else?"

"No, you've done more than enough. I owe you forever."

He shook his head to say no but didn't bother speaking. The two-seater was several inches too small for his long body and his legs hung over the edge.

"Use the bed, please. I'm not even tired." It was a lie, but whatever.

"No, thanks. It's fine once you get comfortable."

"You don't get comfortable like that—you're gonna mess up your spine. What am I going to do with you if you're all hunched over?"

He laid an arm across his eyes, blocking out the light. A yawn stretched and faded his voice.

"It's not bad. Promise."

Determined, she got up and limped to the bed. Stripping the top blanket, she threw it across his body and tucked in the edges.

"What are you doing?"

She grabbed a spare pillow and showed it to him.

"Lift your head."

He obeyed.

"There. At least use this if you're going to be stubborn."

"I've always liked getting tucked in," he said.

"Shut up." She smirked, tried not to laugh.

"Don't get used to it," she said.

She returned to the bed, energy drink in hand. It was early and the balance was a careful one. Without her pills, sleep would continue to evade her until she fell over from exhaustion, but she needed to be mentally sharp for the night ahead. Being wired all night was better than drowsy and barely conscious.

"Hey, T."

"Yeah."

"Will you read me a bedtime story?"

"Shut up."

It was quiet long enough she thought he must be asleep. Other guests moved about their rooms, opening drawers, slamming doors in the hallway. Traffic was a dull hum in the distance, traveling east or west on the highway, almost inaudible through double-paned glass. The city looked familiar with dusk coming soon. Twinkling lights in the distance disappearing into the foothills, but it also looked different from this angle. A difference that made her nervous.

"It's going to be alright." His voice broke the spell of darkness.

"I know," she said, not knowing how that could be true.

By the glow of her phone, Teri searched for information on the missing woman. Hair tangled and wet, fresh clothes loose but comfortable, she curled in a ball near the headboard, scrolling through page after page. Nothing she looked up came back with new information. Without a name, she was searching in the dark, hoping to stumble across something meaningful. None of the ties to Roman led back to the woman she'd seen in his kitchen. She was just missing.

Tireless, she kept up the search until the battery monitor started blinking. After three a.m. it ran out.

Ch. 15

Three heavy-fisted bangs on the door made Teri's chest clench as she struggled to hold her composure. Already up and making coffee, she set down the half-full cup, that was trembling in her hand. Thomas had gone out for breakfast—it had to be him, but instinct and good sense battled as she edged toward the door and peephole. She was trying to position herself to see anything but black when he spoke from the other side.

"It's me, forgot the key card."

She flipped the latch, letting him in.

"Sorry if I scared you. I thought you'd be sleeping."

"I won't ever sleep again. You scared the shit out of me."

He shrugged.

"Sorry."

She smelled fresh biscuits, savory sausage and something sweet.

"Definitely in charge of food. Can you do my grocery shopping from now on?"

He shrugged again, bringing the bags to the table. Their dining area for breakfast, lunch and dinner had become the centerpiece of the room. It was cozy even if it was small.

"I could, but then you'd have to eat something other than frozen burritos. This feast is a product of necessity."

He reached into the bag, retrieved a wrapper spotted with grease and tossed it to her. It smelled amazing.

"We have to keep our strength up. Who knows what's coming today?"

"I had an idea about that," she said.

She savored the first bite, warm and crumbly, only a little burned with a dab of butter on top.

"You know ... making the perfect sausage biscuit is an art form. You can burn it, or worse, you can undercook it and they're all doughy inside. It's hard to get right."

"Parkwood, only place that does it right. What's your idea?"

She licked her fingers, taking a breath.

"You went all the way to Parkwood ... why?"

"Had to check on something. What was your idea?"

She eyed him with suspicion.

"Tell me you didn't go back."

The answer was clear before he spoke. His eyes moved to the side, a twitch when he wanted to lie.

"I didn't go in."

"Shouldn't have gone at all. It's dangerous."

"I don't think it is," he said.

She set the biscuit down, wiping crumbs from her mouth.

"How do you figure?"

"It was normal, empty. No police tape, no one hanging around. I sat across the road for half an hour and there wasn't another car in sight. What did you say the cruiser looked like?"

"It was dark—black, maybe gray. Unmarked."

"Wasn't there. The lot out front was empty."

She paused, considering.

"Doesn't mean it's safe."

"I'm telling you, if they were looking for you, if you were a fugitive, wouldn't there be someone watching the building? A car coming by every now and then, something? It's not on the news, I checked. If there was a body up there, which would definitely stink by now, why's the car gone?"

He took a bite of his own biscuit, let her chew on the facts for a second.

"I think he stumbled out of there as soon as he realized you got the best of him, and he hauled ass. If you show up down the road, it could cause all kinds of problems."

"If I show up, he'll say I resisted arrest or I attacked him or anything. No one can deny it. There's enough drugs in that apartment to put me away for years."

"They're all prescribed to you. No one can prove you're selling that."

"It's on my hard drive. Besides, there was half an ounce pot on the desk before we crashed over it. That's enough for an arrest, and trust me, with these people that's all they need."

He considered her statement, leaned back against the chair.

"He shot the hard drive."

"He shot the tower. If he's smart, he took it with him."

Thomas shook his head, brushing the conversation aside.

"Point is, I don't think they're looking for you. I don't think anyone knows what happened except us, that cop and Roman. I'm not saying you should go back over there, but—"

"We have to go back."

His head cocked; she knew it didn't make sense.

"If it's really safe, I need my clothes, I need my ID and if we're going to find out who this woman is, I can't go through DTs. I need my medication."

"I didn't say it was safe."

"But no one's looking."

"It doesn't *seem* like it."

She could tell he was caught off guard by the sudden shift, but her reasons were good ones.

"So let's do this before they start. The only reason that giant piece of shit wouldn't have the whole place locked down is if he thinks he has as much to lose as I do. If I'm right, he won't let that go on for too long. He'll find a way to get rid of his problem."

She actually *wanted* to go on her own, but since he was the driver, it would take more convincing.

"We need evidence, right? If I can get back in, I think I can come up with something."

"Like what?"

"Just trust me, please."

"What if it's a trap? We'd be defenseless."

"I'd be defenseless, maybe, but it wouldn't matter, because you'll be outside keeping watch."

He blanched.

"There's no way I'm letting you go in there alone."

She hated doing it, but it was time for the big guns.

"Have you ever taken Ambien?"

He shook his head.

"No."

"I've been on it for a year. If I stop, I could have a seizure, I could go into cardiac arrest."

His face screwed up, reading her eyes.

"Are you serious?"

She was, but it would take more than a few days to happen.

"Dead serious."

He considered that. It was the tipping point.

"Fine, I'll go in."

"I won't tell you where it is." She crossed her arms over her chest, pushed away from the table.

"You're not being reasonable, T."

"You've done enough. I'm not putting you in more danger because of me. Do it my way or I'll go alone."

Her only option was a ride share, but her phone was dead and her wallet in a purse in her apartment. If the jerk hadn't stolen it. Thomas took the bluff.

"Fine. If anything, *anything* looks strange, we bolt. No questions."

"Scout's honor," she said.

"You weren't a Scout."

She smirked. "Ate a brownie once."

"That's disgusting."

The street was empty when they arrived. Parked in a lot opposite the building, they could see both directions. It appeared to be a normal morning. Just shy of lunchtime, Thomas had insisted they drive by once, circle the block and come back again. Now holding the door handle, she watched for anything suspicious.

"Looks clear," she said.

"Five more minutes."

"We've been here ten. Let's go before someone shows up."

He didn't answer, but focused on the front entrance, he nodded, signaling approval. She rolled her eyes as soon as he couldn't see. He was just trying to keep her safe.

The air was cold in the shadows where they parked, but a stripe of sun across the street promised warmer temperatures on the other side. She set off at a quick pace, eager to get this over with.

A dark brown car turned off the main road and onto hers the same instant her feet touched sidewalk, the first on this road since they arrived. Exposed, she froze and averted her gaze while the wide old vehicle trundled over potholes at low speed. The car approached, all suspension creaks and brake noise, while she pretended to look for something in a pocket, body turned away. She refused to look at Thomas, who would motion her back to safety. The old monster cruised by, a trail of exhaust from the tailpipe. At the corner it turned and disappeared.

Relieved, she held up a hand in an "It's all right gesture" without looking back and started across the street. The building was quiet in the daytime, one of her favorite features. Everyone she knew of worked, which meant afternoons were a peaceful time to spend at home. Even if you didn't want to.

Gravel crunched underfoot as she approached. The heavy wood door of the building had been painted several times but still managed to chip around the edges. The handle, maybe brass once, was just dark and corroded. She opened it with a metal click, waited for SWAT teams to burst out and tackle her. When nothing happened, she stepped in.

The lobby was empty. *Thump chink thump chink* as she crossed the tile floor. The elevator rattled and clanged announcing its arrival, punctuated by an incongruous *ding* when the car came to a stop. The doors shuttered open. She stepped in and pressed three, ignoring the cramped space. So far so good. It could have been the handful of pills she'd swallowed before they left, but she rode up thinking she felt pretty good, all things considered. Everything hurt, but that wasn't new, and she only had to lean a little bit on her good leg to keep what was now a stinging pain at bay. It could be worse.

The carpet in the elevator was sour and holding her nose didn't keep the stink from crawling up her nose. It smelled like Vegas but without the good parts. When the car came to a stop, she eased forward, anxious for a breath of fresh air. The whole thing jerked, then clanged like metal breaking and did nothing. On the right floor, she checked for the door-open button a second before the ancient machinery kicked in gear and slid free. She hurried out, cussing the rickety death trap.

At the end of the hall, hanging from its frame, her apartment door was splintered beyond repair. A gap large enough to walk through showed even more damage than the last time she'd seen it. The space was irregular and the angle didn't reveal enough to tell if anyone waited to finish the job.

Closer, the debris field that had once been her home was easier to see, though no less difficult to take in. The desk, still standing, was the only intact item. Cables stretched like dead snakes from where the tower had been, its smoldering corpse removed. Shattered glass and ceramic littered the floor, tiny shards poking the air. Everything she owned had been scattered like someone had picked up the room and shook.

When she edged inside the door, it protested but swung open on its own. The couch cushions were torn and tossed aside. Books and magazines lay facedown open on the floor. No one ambushed her from the bedroom or the kitchen, but items that had once been in both were now strewn across the floor. Her clothes, including pants and underwear, trailed from one room to another. It chilled her more that Wallace had been in her personal belongings than caused this much damage on the way out.

The devastation was all-encompassing. Was he looking for something, or was this a tantrum, another message to be delivered, this time more personal? Whatever the motivation, the man she'd left for dead had left no stone unturned ravaging her personal space. Drawers hung open in the kitchen, silverware on the floor. Glasses shattered one by one. She poked through the remnants and considered it an acceptable loss. Small price to pay for your life.

The bedroom looked worse than the rest, with the bed slid to one side, mattress hanging off the frame. The box spring was full of holes. Her nightstand was upended, contents spilled across the floor under a window whose curtain had been ripped free. She looked down on the parking lot across the street, barely visible from this angle. The Camry waited, no sign of danger. Like she'd thought, Wallace hadn't known where to look for the laptop. She stepped over piles of broken things to an open closet where clothes had been pulled from their hangers. In the bottom, the top of a black backpack poked out. She wrestled it free and set it on the leaning mattress. Inside, in a back pocket was a travel-sized laptop. It was a backup that she used for trips and long doctor's visits. One she hadn't used in months. The screen was intact with the power cables nestled beneath the machine in the bottom of its pouch. She was one for one on fail-safes, hoping the second would still pan out. Her filthy lake pants with her bank cards and ID inside were buried near the doorway and took a little luck to find. She retrieved the cards, tossed the pants and started filling the pack. Fresh clothes and deodorant went in next, followed by her toothbrush from its spot in the bathroom cabinet, which had been torn free so it hung from one corner on the wall.

Her heart sank in the main room when she realized every box and bottle of lifesaving prescriptions was gone. Aside from the computer, they were the only thing missing. She'd expected this, but that didn't make the truth any easier. Her customers would find other sources, and most of her medications were ineffective, prescriptions she kept only to sell, but Adderall, Ambien, she needed those. Without them, she had days at best before she would need to check into a hospital to request a refill. The system locked down when a patient tried to get controlled narcotics before the refill date. Standard practice was to treat everyone like a junkie. Better to send an innocent patient through withdrawal than risk that kind of exposure. The irony being there was no way she could afford both drugs at street prices.

"Asshole." She kicked an empty drink bottle into the next room.

The desk drawers were pulled out, but they had been dumped on the floor. She rummaged through contents, hoping for anything. The weed was gone, the pipe too, unless it was part of the glass confetti ground into the floor. Near the bottom she found a green plastic pill organizer. The one she kept for daily doses. Most of the squares had been popped open, but two were closed. Both had pills inside. Two days.

"Super." She thanked her stars again, small favors, and stuffed the pill carrier in the pack. Thinking better of it, she retrieved an Addie, dry swallowed and dropped the container back in. When the horn honked, she almost choked. Reverberating off the hollows of the building and empty lots, it scared her out of her skin. At the window in an instant: the car was still there, Thomas waiting, no one in sight. He was getting antsy. It was a good time to agree with him and get of there.

Nothing else worth saving, she kicked through the shambles of a former life and dragged the door shut. It would never close again, wedged in the space, door handle loose and lock destroyed. The best she could do was hold it in place. Screw it, if someone wanted to rob her, go for it. If they wanted to see the remnants of her old life, step right up.

In the lobby, she felt like it was time to move on. If she got out of this, she would find a better place across town. Someplace that smelled better. Someplace with an elevator that worked. Lost in thought, she hadn't noticed the downstairs neighbor step out of her apartment. A cloud of cigarette smoke, foul and stale, chased her into the lobby and grabbed Teri's attention.

"Hey, girl," the woman said in a gravelly voice. "Three B, right?"

She halted, turned on her heel and faced the woman, who in baggy sweats and a white tank, with stringy blond hair hanging down, didn't look much worse off than she did at the moment, maybe better. The woman had a soda bottle, but she doubted there was soda in it. Ashley, or Aston, something like that, had invited her for "happy hour" when Teri first moved in. Aside from a stale joint and a six-pack, the two had had nothing in common. The woman had even forgotten her name.

"Yeah, Teri," she said.

"That's right," the woman responded as if confirming the answer. They stood apart, Teri making no moves to close the gap, which was only ten feet at most.

The woman checked over her shoulder and slid into the hall, shutting the door behind her. She stood close enough to whisper, clouding the air with years of Marlboro Reds.

"I wanted to say something. Hope you don't mind."

When she didn't respond, the woman continued unfazed.

"I heard what happened. With that guy, ya know?"

Muscles down her spine clenched so tight she thought they might break her back. She studied the woman's eyes. They seemed sincere, if vacant. What had she heard?

"Look, I'm sorry," she said, and placed a hand on Teri's arm.

"I know ... what it's like. You know? So, I won't get in your business, but if you need anything. Anything at all, you let me know."

She had a hard time focusing on the woman's words of support through the cloud that hung about her—it definitely wasn't soda in the bottle. She gawked, caught off guard by the sympathy. What did she think had happened? With the hand still resting on her arm, Teri had a chance to notice the woman's slight figure; she hid it well enough, but she was near skeletal under loose clothes. Her shoulders and arms were nearly all bone. The least likely person to be offering someone else assistance. She didn't have time to think about it, because the woman kept talking, stepping into her personal space.

"Between you and me, I don't think he'll be back."

"No?" she said.

"He took some stuff. Maybe it was yours, maybe it was his. Who cares, right? But you tore him up pretty good. Guy like that, it's gonna hurt his pride. He'll try to play it off, move on to some other poor chick."

"Unless he wants revenge," Teri said.

"I see him around here again, I'll call the cops for you. He won't get in this building."

"Thanks," she said, hoping it was time to leave.

"You did him up, girl. Impressive … with the cane and everything. Good job. You don't take no shit off no one. You show 'em who's boss."

"I'll do that. Thanks," she said, and turned to leave.

The woman let her go but kept talking as she reached for the door.

"I went up there, you know, after. I didn't take nothin'. I'm not like that but just, you know, curious. You don't have to pay for that, girl. I'll tell the super what happened. He's a good guy. That ain't your fault. Ought to sue that jerk you were with, make him fix it."

Teri turned back.

"Did anyone else go up after I left?"

"Like the police?"

"Sure, yeah."

"No one. Not that I saw. Police ain't coming out here. I called 'em, said someone was sneaking around my window, took 'em two hours to come by. I said don't worry 'bout it, I took care of it. Let 'em figure out what that means." The woman pointed two fingers like a gun.

Conversation exhausted, the woman turned back to her apartment and let herself in. Teri watched the woman go, thankful for the news Officer Wallace was still alive, if not exactly excited about it.

The gravelly voice was talking again before her blond head poked out.

"Oh, hey, I got your cat."

"What?"

"Yeah, he was outside there, guess he got out when ... well, you know. Anyway, I got him. I fed him some tuna and he's happy. Just hanging out with my guys, ya know?"

She stared, not sure what to say. She hadn't owned a cat since she was twelve.

"They don't like him sharing the litter box, but hey ... he's company, right?"

This woman was completely off her rocker.

"You wanna see him? He's right inside."

"Uh, no thanks. Look, I really gotta go right now, but can you keep an eye on him for me, for a few days? I'll come by and pick him up."

"Absolutely, yeah, girl. You do what you got to do. He's safe with me."

"I appreciate that," she said, making a note to look for apartments with a pet policy.

"I'm Ashley!" she called as Teri pushed through the door.

"Nice to meet you ... again," Teri said.

Once outside, she hustled out of the parking lot and across the street.

Thomas waited, performing surveillance in both directions on her approach.

"What took you?" he said when she got in.

"Getting info."

"Anything good?"

"I'm not sure yet."

Ch. 16

Leaned over the laptop, fingers clicking keys at rapid speed, she held her breath hoping for one more score. The laptop was fine; it was slower than her PC, but it booted without an issue. Now she was logged into a server farm looking through a list of folders she stored offline. As long as the files had a chance to back up before her tower bit the dust, she had a shot. A shot that might make all the difference.

"Come on … come on," she said under her breath.

"What are you looking for?"

"One sec. Don't jinx it."

She entered her username and password to a secure directory. Her fingers tapped on hard plastic while she waited for the log-in screen. When the page popped up, she searched for "SurvFolder1." When it appeared, she sorted folders by date.

"Yes!" she shouted. "I got it."

Thomas pulled up a chair, leaning over her shoulder.

"Great, what is it?"

"The video. It's everything I got before he cut the feed."

He leaned in, reading the list of files with nonsense titles.

"That's awesome. Can it help us?"

She sighed.

"Well, some. It shows him cleaning up the murder. It's not hard evidence, but it'll definitely work in our favor and it gives us a firm timeline."

"That's good."

"Also, he doesn't know we have it. They think everything was on the hard drive."

She started typing again, pulling up a terminal window. The cursor blinked, waited, then returned a message:

Address not found. Try again in 30 seconds.

The timer started the countdown on its own. The program would keep doing that until it found a connection. Oh well, two for three was pretty good.

"The feed is still down, but we can use this. Maybe I can blow it up and make out something useful. Point is, we're at least back where we started."

If he thought she was reaching, that would be fair, but she had to hold out hope for a breakthrough. Until something better turned up, they had the video and the chance that something critical had been overlooked. She opened the latest recording and scrubbed through the tape, stopping at key points, while Thomas paced back and forth. She stopped near the end when the first cops arrived.

"Wait. Pause that."

She stopped the frame as the two officers filed into the hallway.

"I know that guy."

"He the one that picked you up?" she said.

"No. He was at the station. He's the one that questioned me when I got there." A finger landed on the screen, pointing out the cowboy cop who got friendly with Roman.

"He's the one I told everything to."

"What about the ones who arrested you?"

"Didn't believe me. When I argued with them, they called it resisting arrest, put me in cuffs. That guy came in after."

"Did you get his name?"

"Naw. But I didn't think he believed me either. Just asked a bunch of questions and left."

They stared at the screen, the erect figure, thumbs tucked, holding watch by the front door.

"You're not gonna like the rest of this, then."

She fast-forwarded the recording to the end, let it play when the man in blue shook Roman's hand, a friendly word between them.

"How many cops does he know?"

"At least two," she said. "Probably more."

Thomas massaged the bridge of his nose, walking away.

"Nothing's going to stick to this guy. We're outgunned here."

"No one is unreachable," she said, and pushed away from the table. It had been an hour and her butt hurt from sitting. She grabbed the pack off the bed and walked to the bathroom. Her foot felt better. Especially with an industrial-grade pain reliever from her pill pack.

"Where you goin'?"

She shook the bag.

"To take a shower. I do that now."

The hotel water was warm in seconds. Standing under the showerhead, she let the heat soak into her body, like warm hands kneading the tension from her shoulders. She let it wash over her face, through her hair and down her neck and back. A river of heat that traveled down her aching spine. It spread through her limbs until her entire body was alive and red from its touch.

By the time she lathered her scalp with two guest-sized shampoo bottles, the entire room was filled with steam. It made her tingle. The tips of her fingers, her skin. Her nerve endings, didn't do well in heat, but it worked wonders on aching joints. A constant trade-off. A sweet floral aroma with tea tree filled her senses, added a different tingle to her head and hands that distracted from the spreading numbness. She lowered the temperature and slid back under the showerhead, letting it pour over and wash suds into the molded tub floor.

It was a moment. A single pleasant experience in an ocean of the unbearable. She gave herself to it and let nothing disturb the purity. The drumming of the heavy droplets sounded like distant words she couldn't make out. Her ears popped and she realized someone was shouting. It was Thomas.

She wrenched off the water, straining to hear. Waited for it to come again.

"Teri, check this out."

He was outside the door now. Close enough it made her jump.

"Just a sec."

From the tone in his voice, he was worked up over something. She dressed in a hurry, threw the towel over her head and rushed into the room, which was ice-cold with the air conditioner running. A cloud of steam and the scent of free shampoo close behind.

"What's going on?" Thomas was sitting at the table, laptop open. He turned the screen and she stopped. He was watching a view of the kitchen with no one in frame.

"Did you find something?"

"It's live," he said, pushing back from the table.

"What?"

"I don't know when it started, but I checked the window and it's live. No one's home but look."

He pointed out a time stamp on the window. He was right, the feed was live.

"Are the others up too?"

"I don't know how to check that."

She shooed him aside and pulled the other IPs from her list. One by one, the windows popped up, all dark. The same message on each one.

"Why just this one?" she said.

"No idea. It was just like that."

They watched together while rivulets of chilled water ran down her neck. Minutes passed. Nothing changed. Her heart sank, but the feed was live, which meant someone had turned it on.

"All right. Let's see what happens."

She turned the laptop so it was visible from the bed and padded over. Propping pillows behind her, she patted the mattress.

"Come on, sit with me."

"What are we doing?" he asked.

She motioned to the small screen glowing across the room.

"Watching TV."

"I've seen this one," he said.

He picked up the computer and set it at the end of the bed.

"Your eyes are better than mine."

Fluffing the other pillow, he climbed into bed next to her and got comfortable. They watched the screen together until it timed out. Teri kicked the laptop with her foot, bringing the image back.

"Why would just one camera go back on?" he asked.

"I don't know. Maybe he's taunting us."

She didn't think that was true, but what explanation was there?

He stared at the screen; unchanging, it could have been a picture.

"You do this for fun?" he said.

"Well, when I do it, there's people on it."

"You should get out more."

"No thanks, those weirdos are out there. Once you've seen someone in private, you get a whole new understanding of who they really are."

She pushed her pillow under his arm and scooted down so she was leaning against his chest.

"This OK?" she said.

It wasn't the first time they'd lain like that. Watching movies on her couch, he was the designated pillow. Besides, she wanted someone close right now, and that didn't feel wrong.

"It's fine. Can you see?" His arm limp behind her, his hand brushed her back as she curled up.

"Don't need to. Watch for a bit. Wake me up if it changes."

He wiggled in place, settled into position.

"Go for it."

She closed her eyes, willing her body to release the tension it had refused to let go of. She didn't have answers and didn't try to come up with any. For now she just was, resting, letting the will to keep going find her when it would. Minutes passed until her bones settled in. The room was cool, the only sound the air conditioner and their breathing. Hers slow and steady, his louder and even paced. She shifted. Her arm brushed his, her hands tucked back away toward her chest.

"Teri."

"Mm-hmm," she said, sinking deeper into him.

"Something's happening."

She lifted her head, eyes still closed.

"What?"

"Look."

He pulled his arm free, reached down and scooped up the laptop. When she pulled herself up, he placed the computer on her lap. She didn't understand what was happening until Hayley came on-screen.

Alone in the kitchen, Roman's daughter stood behind the island facing the camera. She held a notebook with black Sharpie letters taking up the whole page.

I can help you.

Under that was a phone number.

"What the shit," Thomas said.

"Give me your phone."

"Hold on a second. Isn't this ... convenient?"

Teri watched the girl on the screen holding up a pad, eyes wide, desperate. She looked older than fifteen now. A deep sadness had taken root in her features. She looked over her shoulder every few seconds, head cocked, listening.

"She's afraid, look."

Thomas watched her movements, suspicion etched deep.

"I don't like it."

Hayley's silent vigil lasted until Teri couldn't bear watching. At once, the girl shut the book and hurried offscreen. Moments after she was gone, a shadow passed through the frame. One Teri recognized. If the other feed were live, Roman's broad shoulders would be seen lumbering toward the living room.

She looked at Thomas, hoping for agreement. She received doubt.

"What do you think?" she said.

"Too easy. Doesn't make sense."

She pushed away, facing him head-on.

"Why not?"

"She has no reason to help us. She doesn't even know us. Why would she risk it?"

"Have you seen him? Look at her, she's terrified."

"Feels like a trap."

He pushed off the bed, crossed the room. She persisted.

"Yeah, but what if it isn't? Who's in a better spot to give us information than she is? Can we ignore that?"

His reluctance wasn't unexpected. She understood. It might be a trap, but what would a phone call hurt? They would talk to Hayley, see what she knew. Play it safe.

"What if she can help? If she knows who this woman is, what's that worth? We don't have to take any risk."

"Everything is a risk. What if she's a decoy to get us in the open?"

"How would she do that? We just call, pure and simple. Straight talk, no games."

Her arguments were getting nowhere. He didn't trust it and when he dug in, there was no getting him out of it.

"I don't like it."

She picked up the laptop, carrying it to the table. She turned the screen away from the room, empty feed still playing.

"How many chances are we going to get?" she argued.

Posed by the window, looking down on the lot below, he ran a hand over his head.

"I'm not saying do nothing. Alright? Just … wait. Let's see what happens next. If we don't answer, do they try something else?"

She considered the point. It was possible her desire to protect the girl was coloring her emotions. Watching the screen and then Thomas squinting past his own reflection, deep in thought, she relented. It wasn't just her involved. Safety had to be top priority.

"OK, we wait," she said.

"See what happens tomorrow. We have the number," he said.

She pushed the laptop away.

"I'm going for a walk."

"Is that a good idea?"

She shot him a look and grabbed her cane.

"I'll manage."

The walk went as far as the vending machines but this time on the first floor to put some distance between herself and the room. The rented space was feeling smaller by the minute. Armed with her bank card, she hovered before the choices. Stuck whether to pick the caffeine rush and sugar crash of a soda or the sweet gooey goodness of chocolate and caramel, she wasted time weighing the options.

It made sense. It really did—Thomas wanted to be safe and he wanted to keep her safe, but she also knew why he was involved in the first place. Asking him to risk his life by opening a door Roman might come busting through was too much. That didn't mean it wasn't their best chance, maybe their only chance.

She picked chocolate, thought better of it and got the soda too. Screw it, if she had to suffer, might as well do it on a sugar high. Life was too short to have regrets. The candy bar didn't make it past the alcove, devoured while she leaned against the machine, cool on her back as she chewed. Its crumpled wrapper landed in an overflowing trash can in the corner.

The ride up was slow, followed by a slower walk to the room. There was no hurry for the first time in days. It felt good to move without looking over her shoulder. It felt good to have time to think. Surrounded by closed doors, she turned at the end of the hall and slid the key in the door. A new realization was just forming. The choice was always easy; it was the consequence that could be a bitch.

Inside Thomas lay on the couch, TV on, turned low. Trying to look comfortable on the small sofa was absurd. He turned it off when she walked in, sitting up at once.

"Don't stop for me," she said.

"It's crap. Fearmongering and speculation."

"Turn it on, I want to see if anyone is missing yet."

"She came back."

"The girl?"

Teri crossed to the table and took a seat. The feed was empty again.

"Yeah, same message. She stood there for a few minutes like last time, then ran off."

"Makes sense. She doesn't know we're watching or *if* we are. She's probably hitting it at intervals. Whenever he's not around."

"I know. Look, I was thinking. We're not going to get a better chance than this, but I don't want to call from here. Let's go somewhere public. It sounds paranoid, but if maybe they're tracing the line, we don't know."

"Sounds fine. Where?"

"Anywhere. There aren't pay phones anymore, so we'd have to use a cell, but we could do it from a mall parking lot or something."

"You want to go to the mall?"

"No, I definitely do not."

She thought about it. The plan made sense. It offered them some protection and gave them access to a potential ally.

"OK. Let's do it."

She pulled up the video feed from the last thirty minutes. The girl came on-screen just as before, held up the same note and scurried offscreen before Roman appeared. Everything was exactly the same, just as Thomas said.

"You OK?"

She looked up.

"Yeah, sorry."

"You caught the part where I said you're right?"

She paused the video on Hayley, looking terrified and alone. She knew that feeling.

"Yeah, sorry, things on my mind. Let's wait. Give it till tomorrow."

He came over and sat at the table.

"If we do this right, it should be safe enough."

"Yeah, but we only get one chance. Let's be careful."

The relief on his face was masked by confusion.

"OK, tomorrow, then."

"Tomorrow afternoon. If nothing weird happens, we drive to the mall ... or whatever, and we make the call. We'll keep it short."

She closed the laptop and went for the bathroom.

"Gonna brush my teeth."

Faceup on the counter, the phone waited while she brushed. A door unopened. She glared at the screen, sneered and flipped it over. The TV news was back on, returning from commercial break. She pushed the door almost closed. The robotic cadence of voices reading cue cards drifted in.

The number was already in the phone. She had punched it in as soon as she was out of sight. Safe in the bathroom to commit her treason. Since then it waited for her command.

She spit, rinsed and wiped her chin with a towel that smelled better than it felt against her skin. It was good to be clean again. In the mirror, she admired exceptionally straight teeth and did her best to ignore the black device waiting on the counter but it had to be done.

She hit Send but not a call. A text.

Teri: It's me what can you tell us?

Ch. 18

That was that. The choice was made. She wanted to feel guilty, wanted to say it was the wrong thing to do, but that wasn't true. She was taking the reins of fate and taking responsibility for her own situation. Fingers tapped on the counter while she waited. The news was going off, a new show taking its place. Something louder and faster paced. She could hear Thomas moving around on the couch. Seeking comfort that was impossible. Only a sliver of light peaked through the cracked door.

As she strained to make out any movements from the other side, the buzz of an incoming message caught her off guard. It made her jump, sending the toothpaste and several bottles of soap clamoring into the sink. She snatched up the phone, cradled it to her chest to stop any further sounds. How had she forgot to turn off vibrate? It was awhile before her pulse returned to normal. The questions from the next room never came, no sign that he had heard or cared about the sudden racket. She was jumpy and yes, a little guilty. She told herself it wasn't betrayal if she had to protect the only person on her side. Not unforgiveable anyway. She unlocked the screen and turned off vibrate. A new message waited.

Hayley: Are you the girl who saw it?

Too easy. Betraying her friend's trust didn't mean she wouldn't be careful.

Teri: What did I see?

The wait was long enough to consider a lot of things. Whether she had blown it, whether this was a trick. If the girl really was scared and reaching out, she had no assurance Teri wasn't Roman, drawing information from her.

Hayley: He killed that woman, right? Like the cop said.

Unable to stop herself, she fell backward, landing on the toilet. The words burned into the screen verified something critical. She wasn't alone. Someone out there would believe them. On the heels of that realization came something else: This girl was in danger. If she was telling the truth. she was living with a monster. If he found out they were talking, anything could happen. If the girl panicked …

She typed out her response, considering the best approach.

Teri: Yes.

Time between messages faded. The TV played uninterrupted. Her small white room could have been on another planet. She waited, feeling guilty, feeling scared, certain there was a way out and this girl was it. The next message came:

Hayley: Can we meet?

There it was. The bait. Maybe Thomas was right, it was a trap. Sidestepping the question was easy enough.

Teri: What can you tell me now?

Time was passing. How long could she stay in here, fifteen minutes? Five more and she had to leave.

Hayley: I can't tell you anything.

She clutched the phone, fighting the urge to launch it across the room and banged a fist into her leg instead. How could she think this would work? How could she endanger herself and Thomas both and not see it for a trap? She braced herself for the inevitable.

Hayley: But I can show you. I found something. Maybe you can use it.

Three minutes left.

Teri: Tell me.

The girl responded fast.

Hayley: I can't. Not safe.

She stared at the words. Felt their weight. The girl was right, it wasn't safe. You couldn't trust anyone.

Teri: No deal.

Time was up. She slipped the phone in her pocket and stepped into the room. Thomas noticed her when she came in, looking up from the late news.

"Feel better?"

She nodded to the TV.

"Anything?"

"Nothing good and nothing about our missing woman."

Not a surprise. No one was finding out about this unless she made it happen. By the time they realized there was a problem, Roman would be cleaner than the kitchen tiles. The only other person who witnessed what happened that night was on the other end of that camera.

Every minute that passed was time lost. Hayley had sent one more message since their conversation. It stuck in her mind, taunted her.

Trust me.

Who could ask such a thing? She twisted in the sheets until it was clear she wasn't getting any rest and moved to the table.

Even the square surface with enough room for two chairs felt cramped. This room was too small for another day of hiding out.

The feed was live but empty. On Roman's social media page, she pulled up the beach photo again. The girl knew who her father was now; did she know back then? Where did her loyalties lie?

"Anything new?" Thomas said from the couch. The TV was low now, inaudible. He had his phone in his lap.

"Nothing yet. What are you up to?"

He flashed a satellite view of the city at her.

"A lot of these places are fenced off, difficult to access. I think I can figure out where he went. Narrow it down at least. Maybe we can establish a search area."

"Good luck."

"Thanks, gonna need it."

She frowned, a familiar pang striking inside.

"Why don't you take the bed tonight? Switch it up."

"No thanks. I'm going to stay up and work on this."

"You're very stubborn."

"One of my finer qualities. If this call doesn't work out tomorrow, we need a backup plan. Something solid."

"If you change your mind …"

"I'll let you know."

At some point the view changed. Both Roman and Hayley were in the kitchen. They ignored each other. How hadn't she noticed it before, the way the girl slunk by, avoided contact? She moved from fridge to counter to cabinets, always out of the way.

The girl watched his every move but only when his back was turned. When he faced her, she looked away, always avoiding eye contact. She kept the notebook, close, protected. The girl's eyes glanced at the camera, then away again. Teri might have imagined the first one but then two more times.

What if it wasn't a trap? What if it *was*?

She searched for a signal in the girl's behavior to make the decision for her. She saw no malice. What she did see was fear and uncertainty.

Roman left. By herself at the counter, Hayley watched until he was gone and flipped open the book. In black marker she drew a new message in tall letters that filled the page. She didn't have to hold it for Teri to read, but the capital letters tugged at her heart when they turned to the camera.

PLEASE.

She held it up, five seconds, ten; then she closed the book and stared into the camera, notebook clutched again to her chest. Thomas continued on his phone ignoring Teri, searching for a solution that would protect them both. The girl plead with her eyes for a complete stranger to reach out and rescue her. Teri had seen the woman scream with no sound, seconds before she went silent for good.

She tapped out the message and hit Send.

Teri: Tomorrow.

The girl reached for her phone on-screen. She read the message and looked into the lens. Was it hope in her eyes, or deceit?

Hayley: Where?

Teri sent her an address for a diner half a mile away. It would help protect Thomas and give her a chance to look around before approaching the girl.

Teri: Eight a.m.

The girl shot her a thumbs-up and scrawled something in big letters.

Thank You

When she left, Teri closed the lid.

Ch. 19

She woke when the morning was new, still slumbering. Thomas snored on the couch, comforter pulled over his head. Setting an alarm hadn't been necessary or possible but sleep was light, coming in fits. The limited Ambien had kept her from properly dozing off. With the yawning start that places like this had the day was just getting under way. It would be another hour before the commotion reached full tilt. Another thirty minutes or more before Thomas stirred. He had always been a late and heavy sleeper.

Already up for an hour, she lay still, afraid to move or make a sound. When the time came, she slid from under the covers, waiting at the end of the bed, watching his blanket rise and lower in syncopated rhythm. Already dressed, she had only to get out of the room unnoticed, downstairs and across the street. It was a short walk from there.

She gave herself an extra window. Twenty minutes' travel time meant she could reach the diner fifteen minutes early. Enough time to watch the girl arrive, spot anything suspicious before she exposed herself. If anything was off, even a little out of order, she would come back to the room and try again. That's what she told herself. When the room door clicked into place behind her, the light turning from green to red, she almost believed it.

A note left on the nightstand said "Getting air." Not a complete lie. At the bottom it said "Back soon. Don't worry." The questions would come when she got back, but that was a problem for another time.

She was down the hall and on her way to the lobby before she had a chance to change her mind. Outside, the cold front had settled, forcing out thoughts of doubt and fear of failure. Instead she braced herself against the brisk wind that conspired to blow her over as she crossed the half-full parking lot to the road. The effort helped her to steel against the adversity, instead she felt alive, confident and ready to face what lay ahead.

This section of highway, littered with fast-food joints and service stations, served as the front row of an enormous shopping center beyond. It kept traffic heavy and drivers distracted with navigating the awkward lane patterns. There were far too many cars for her to scan each one. She'd have to hope to catch the girl on her way in.

A gas station on her side of the highway made a good lookout point for the diner. At an angle across the four-lane intersection, it was far enough that she could hide in plain sight and still make out who came and went on the other side. Staying back off the road kept her from being noticed if Hayley had thought of the same thing. Since she assumed the girl had no idea what she looked like, the only way Teri could be recognized was if someone else tagged along. Someone like Officer Wallace.

To avoid suspicion, she entered the gas station from the side and went to the cooler. Customers could get away with awkward loitering better than drifters. Leered at the entire way by a woman behind the counter, she brought a bottle of water to the register with a fake smile.

"You buy this?" the woman said.

"Huh?"

"It's water. You can get water for free."

She shrugged.

"Need the bottle."

The woman's eyes trailed down to her leg, her cane, the limp that drew attention.

Don't ask.

She didn't, ringing up the sale.

Teri gave her two ones and took the change. She could see the words form but doubt held the woman back. People were nervous about bringing up her disability. To the woman's credit, she said nothing until Teri was walking out.

"Hope you feel better."

She chuckled at that.

"Yeah, me too."

She *was* thirsty but the water served another purpose. With security cameras all over the building, if something did happen to her during this clandestine meeting, there was video evidence of when and where Teri Fletcher had last been seen alive. That was worth a dollar seventy-five

A row of hedges near the road separated the station from the highway and at the right angle made her invisible from the checkout counter. Posted there, drinking her water, which tasted a lot better than tap, she watched the restaurant. Her phone said it was seven forty. No missed calls, no messages.

Four cars waited in the opposite lot. A white Camaro close to the door in a handicapped space. A blue van, at least ten years old, and a rusted-out work truck that looked as likely to fall apart on the spot as start up again. On the side a small sedan, like a Civic, blue. None of these belonged in the Shores. Hayley wouldn't drive, because the Gardners only had one car, but who she got to bring her could be anyone, including the police.

No one went in or out while she waited. Five minutes till and the scene hadn't changed. Second-guessing at its highest, she was about to step from the hiding spot and risk walking across when a wine-red Mustang pulled in, tinted glass all around. It pulled up to the door but didn't park. Teri thought she could hear the music inside when the passenger door opened. The girl that stepped out couldn't be anyone else. She recognized the slight build, her timid posture even from that distance. As soon as the door shut, the driver was gone in a roar of horsepower and exhaust. *Subtle.* Hayley went straight inside.

Teri watched until the Mustang was gone, speeding down the highway and taking an off-ramp toward the Shores. It was now or never. The intersection was marked and had crossing lights, which made it easy to reach the other side at a casual pace. Coming at the diner head-on seemed like a bad idea, even with the driver long gone. At the sidewalk, she passed the entrance down a short driveway to the mall, crossed farther down and came back from the rear. This gave her time to think about a plan. A plan she realized should have been considered before now. Hayley was already inside, so there would be no way to approach without being seen first. Glass windows covered two walls; the entrance and half of the side section she approached from. It would be a miracle if she wasn't spotted already.

A few feet of brick wall by the dumpsters gave her a moment to pause and set her mind to it. This was it. The lot looked clear, one of the few times she hadn't seen a cop parked out front. No one was following her, or if they were, they did a hell of a good job going unnoticed. Around the corner and down the front walk, she felt like a duck in a shooting gallery, just waiting to get picked off. The smell of car exhaust and coffee mingled in the area out front.

The diner was loud with a double-door entry that helped contain the clang of silverware, the constant rattle of dishes and the clamoring conversation within. Muffled from the outside, inside it was an onslaught of sights and smells, most but not all pleasant. Fresh bacon grease smacked her in the face as soon as the door opened, punctuated by the sickening sweet of syrup and burning waffle batter that gave the place its name. She scanned the room for her contact. It was warm, despite the draft from outside and every table seemed full of strangers whose eyes landed on her, made an appraisal and darted away. Mouths full of chewed food sucked down coffee and fought to be heard over the others. In the back, under the manager's window, Hayley sat by herself in a four-person booth. The girl was watching her, a livewire tension in her eyes.

Teri resisted eye contact, giving herself time to size up the situation. Walking over casual, like she was a customer headed to the restroom, she made a final scan of the diner and the lot outside, found nothing unusual and at the last possible second took a seat in front of the girl.

"Hi, Hayley."

The girl narrowed her eyes, taken back by the familiarity.

"I'm Teri," she continued and offered her hand.

She took it, and then drew her hand back.

"Nice to meet you," Teri offered.

The girl's attention was like a bird, flitting here and there. Frequently it landed on the parking lot, out to the road and then came back to rest on Teri who sat patiently, letting her get comfortable with the situation.

"Nervous?" Teri asked.

Hayley eyed her.

"Aren't you?"

"Very," she admitted.

The girl was fidgety, scratching nails on the underside of the table. Teri asked the question before she could think it over.

"Is someone coming?"

That got a reaction, suddenly present she spoke in a low, unsteady voice.

"No, I'm ... I think he knows."

The fear was contagious, because Teri's muscles tensed at the statement. Determined to play it cool, she assessed the girl. Figured her to be paranoid.

"What does he know ... that you're coming here?"

Already she felt the regret of agreeing to come. Her feet turned toward the door on their own, ready to bolt. Casually, she forced them straight again, intent on not sending any signals of agitation.

"No. No, but I think he knows something. Or that I suspect something. I don't know. He's acting different."

She willed herself to relax, but it only worked a little. Enough that she didn't jump when a waitress dropped a stack of silverware on the table and asked for their drink orders. Teri ordered coffee. Hayley did too.

"You always drink coffee?" Teri asked

"Not really, just ..." She shrugged.

"Understood."

The girl's eyes were red around the edges; she hadn't been sleeping either. Her fingers twitched, clicking fingernails in order, then starting again. Eye contact was erratic, neither willing to focus too long without checking outside. She decided to change her approach.

"Are you OK?" Teri asked.

The answer was direct, no hesitation.

"No. Not at all, but I have to be. I thought you were him, tricking me maybe. Like he found out I hooked the camera back up."

"How did you manage that?" Teri said.

"It was just unplugged. It has like a twist-on part. When it's running, the little light turns on, so I took that apart. It looks like it's still off."

"That's genius."

"I figured that's how you saw it. What the cops said, it didn't make sense until he turned those off. Then I figured, somehow … you were spying, I guess?"

Teri's face flushed.

"Sorry."

"I don't care, whatever. Anyway, you're lucky. I thought he'd get rid of you by now. He's resourceful, you don't know how many friends he has."

"He tried. It was close," Teri said.

It felt weird discussing her father in such a negative light. As far as Teri knew the girl had no other family.

Hayley studied her and went on.

"He won't stop. He had me followed to school."

She didn't know how to respond to that, but the girl's posture, even as scared as she was, was mature and intelligent. She knew what she was up against. This girl was brave, resilient. Teri wanted to tell her everything was going to be all right, but it seemed now maybe that should go the other way.

"Did you see it?" Hayley asked.

Her mouth went dry. On cue a pair of mugs hit the table, filled to the brim with black coffee. She stirred in a sugar packet and a couple of creamers. Hayley took three.

"Yes, I did," she said at last.

"So, he really did it?"

She nodded.

"Are you sure she's dead?"

She nodded.

"Positive."

The news wasn't a shock to the girl, not on the outside at least. It was a confirmation, Teri suspected something the girl needed to make her next move. A hand went in her jacket pocket and pulled out a small piece of black plastic.

"I found this." She slid it across the table.

It was a USB drive, no bigger than a thumbnail, with a little cord attached. Teri reached out and covered it, picked it up, cradled it in her palm.

"Where did you find this?"

"Those cops, they looked in the garage, but they weren't going to find anything. After he went to work, I went out there. It was clean, but this was in the driveway. No one ever looked there. It was hers—it has her name and a bunch of files on it."

She rubbed the device between her fingers, rigid plastic, cold metal. This tiny thing was worth dying for. It had her name on it.

"What was her na—"

Hayley interrupted.

"Who's that?"

When she turned, a black Camry pulled into the first space by the door. The driver, obscured behind a lowered visor, killed the engine and waited. One hand on the wheel, the other rubbed a chin of fresh stubble.

"He's driven by twice," Hayley said.

"Shit."

The girl was bowed like a cat, her hand already resting on the corner of the table, ready to launch herself at a moment's notice. She eyed Teri.

"Friend of yours?"

"Maybe not anymore. Sit tight … and please don't leave."

When Hayley agreed, Teri got up and walked back into the cold and eerily quiet morning. Thomas nodded as she passed in front of the car, nothing more. Around to the driver's side, she waited for the window to lower.

"I'm sorry," she said, hoping to head off some of the disappointment, the anger.

His voice was flat, not angry, not sad. Just business.

"That her?"

She nodded. "Yeah."

He scanned the parking lot, looking over both shoulders.

"What did she say?"

"She found this." Teri held the drive out where he could see it.

"Good, get in. Let's go."

"I can't."

The calm left. Caretaking took its place.

"What else can she do for us? Do you know how dangerous this is?"

"Yes, I do, and that's why I didn't want you here."

Those were the wrong words, but they were true.

"Well, I'm here. So let's go before something bad happens."

"She's terrified. That girl isn't any kind of decoy. She's scared and she needs our help."

"We need help. What if she was followed? She might not even realize it. This is a bad idea. We need to go, please. Now."

"I'm going back. She needs us." The words were firm. She turned and went back toward the door. She heard him get out, heard the door shut, harder than normal, but otherwise he kept his composure. They said nothing as they walked in together, Thomas holding the door for her. Confused, the girl stood to leave before Teri introduced him.

"This is Thomas. He's my friend. You can trust him."

It was clear she didn't, but she took a seat again.

"Hello," he said.

She nodded back.

"Hi."

"Great," Teri said.

All seated, Thomas on the inside, uncomfortable and doing a bad job hiding it, she tried again.

"Hayley, who was the woman that had this?"

She shrugged, a pained look on her face.

"I don't know. She came over sometimes. She was gone when I got home most of the time, but I could smell her perfume and he was always in a good mood. I figured it out."

"You met her?" Thomas said.

"One time. She was sweet. Pretty, I liked her."

"You said her name was on this?" Teri said, holding up the drive.

"Yeah, Angela. I don't know where she worked or anything, but I looked on there, and there's a lot of stuff with my dad's name on it. Some emails, stuff like that. I tried to look it up, but it doesn't make any sense. I thought maybe, you can hack webcams, you could figure this out?"

"It's different, but I'll try," she said.

Hayley continued to fidget, sipped her coffee. It was clear their time was short. Thomas spoke.

"Do you know where your dad went that night?"

She shook her head.

"Didn't know he did until later. I saw her car leave, thought she was driving."

"What did she drive?"

"Escalade, I think? It was big like that. Black. New, real new."

"She had money," Thomas said.

Teri frowned at him. She wanted to read this drive. She wanted her computer right now. Why hadn't she thought to bring it?

"Did you notice anything else?"

Thomas hadn't looked at her since they sat down, but he was asking all the right questions, and his tone remained even, non-threatening.

"Nothing really. He's calm. It's creepy when he talks to me. I know he should be worried, but it's not there. He doesn't think anyone can touch him."

"Let's hope he's wrong," he said.

The girl may have frowned; it was her father they were talking about. Otherwise she was very together for a girl in her position. It made Teri wonder how kids could handle so much stress.

"Thank you, for doing this. It can't be easy," she said.

"What else could I do?"

"Hayley, where's your mother?" Thomas asked.

The question should have caught her off guard, but Hayley seemed impossible to surprise.

"You mean did he kill her too? No, she's just … gone."

"How do you mean?"

"She had problems, addictions or whatever. He sent her to rehab and then when she came out—" The girl shrugged. "I don't know, I don't see her anymore."

"That sucks."

"It's OK."

"Do you need a ride somewhere?" Thomas offered.

"No, thanks. I'm ditching today. I'll find somewhere to be."

"You have my number," Teri said. She didn't look, but she figured that would an earn a sideways glance from Thomas.

Hayley nodded again.

"We should go." He tapped her knee and they slid out of the booth.

"We'll do everything we can," Teri said. "Promise."

"Thanks. I'll let you know if anything changes at home."

"Great."

Back in the car, Teri took her seat and buckled in without speaking. Thomas started the car, let the engine idle.

"I'm sorry, I had to … I didn't want you to get more involved."

"I know why," he said. "Promise me you'll never do that again. "

He sighed.

"I'm invested here, all in and I can't protect you if I can't trust you."

"Prote—"

She let it go.

"Yeah. OK."

"Promise?"

"Promise."

Ch. 20

Teri plugged in the USB while Thomas pulled up a chair. They sat shoulder to shoulder as the window came up.

"Wait … can they track this?"

She held up her hands. *Probably* …

"Forget it, what's on there?"

She clicked open the folder and scrolled through the contents.

"It's files. PDFs of documents mostly. Looks like some emails too. There's a lot of files here."

She scrolled through a list that must have contained at least a hundred separate icons. Each one a thumbnail of a scanned official-looking document. She opened one. A sheet with rows of numbers and dollar amounts down the right-hand side. No company name or header of any kind to identify their purpose.

"I don't know what this is. It's a form. A ledger sheet maybe."

Thomas leaned in closer.

"It's tracking money, that's for sure. I don't know, try another one."

The next one was the same form with different numbers.

"It's a payroll maybe?"

Whatever their purpose, the sheets were cryptic beyond recognition. They looked like part of an Excel sheet had been copied, but with none of the data that helped decode its purpose. Every one was the same, alphanumeric entries down the left side, dollar amounts on the right, but they didn't add up to anything. There were dates ranging back at least two years, one per line.

"Doesn't make sense," she said.

"That's what Hayley said, but we can figure this out. Maybe these are bank accounts, and the ones on the right are balances."

"OK, but whose accounts and why?"

Another page more of the same, no new clues.

"Check the emails."

A series of emails, twenty in all, populated the bottom of the list. They were all saved from a single address with a number that could have been a date code. The first read: *A.Hoff@SpryteMail.com_01-15*. She opened it.

From: B. Smitz

To: A. Hoffman

Subject: Re: FWD: communication R. Gardner to M. Daly

Maurice,

Approve C10 with previous conditions.

No confirm necessary.

Thanks.

R.

The email was part of a chain forwarded from Angela's account. There was a reply at the bottom.

Angela,
Can we confirm C10 is Central Project?
Brian

Below that:

No confirmation. Yet. Will keep looking.

The chain ended there. She opened the next set.

From: A. Hoffman
To: B. Smitz
Subject: FWD: R. Gardner - M. Daly
Maurice,
Please inform Mr. James that contributions should be made by check to campaign fund directly. For tracking purposes.
R.

The remaining messages read the same way. Most referenced C10 or the Central Project, some just naming "the project," but none explained what that was or why it was worth killing over.

"So, she's been copying his emails and sending them to this guy Brian. There's about ten tons of ledgers or what look like ledgers and some kind of project that I've never heard of and neither have you," Thomas said.

"That's about it, yes."

"So … how does this help us?"

"Like this."

They needed a new tactic. With a name now, they could find out who Angela was and piece together the puzzle of why she was at Roman's and what she was looking for.

Teri typed "Angela Hoffman Asheville" into the search bar and hit Enter.

"Fingers crossed," she said, and realized that hers already were. A list of promising results faced them.

The first was a LinkedIn profile for an Angie Hoffman, the second an address search with similar names. She made a note to come back to that one. Down the page was a link that read:

COA Award Winners Share Spotlight in Downtown Gala

Below that was a description listing Angela Hoffman as a winner. She clicked the link.

The page was a news article announcing a list of recipients for the City of Asheville's "Spirit of Hope" award. The page listed names of the prizewinners next to their field of service. Angela's name appeared near the bottom.

"What'd she do?" Thomas asked.

Teri read the notation out loud.

"Angela Hoffman, City Attorney's Office—excellence in community welfare initiatives."

"Seriously?"

"That's what it says."

Thomas ran his hands over his face, groaning.

"This gets better every day. Is there any good news in there?"

"None so far."

Thomas stood up, paced the room. He went to the window, peeked through the curtains like he expected a SWAT team to show up.

"Is that her?" he asked.

"Only one way to find out," she said.

They pulled up the city attorney website and navigated to staff. A row of photographs had titles beside them. The city attorney and executive attorney were followed by a list of assistants. She didn't need the name to know she was right when she landed on a picture of a young woman with dark hair and a bright smile. Next to the picture was Assistant City Attorney, Angela Hoffman. It was her, same smile, same confident attitude. In the picture she looked no older than thirty.

"Shit."

"That doesn't make sense," Thomas said. "If she's assistant attorney, why is no one looking for her? It's not even on the news."

Teri saved the woman's picture and closed the page.

"Good question."

She went back to the search results and opened the next link.

"The better question is what the assistant city attorney was doing in Roman Gardner's kitchen, snooping through his files and getting handsy with her killer."

"Doesn't make sense," he said again.

"Let's found out who we're dealing with."

The next page was a news report on a local marathon. The same runners from Roman's page were posing for cameras with huge banners that read "Run for Your Life." A shot like the one on his page was at the bottom. This one was different, including a caption.

"This one has names on it," she said.

"That would have been useful before."

She read the names. The other two runners were the city attorney himself and another assistant. The caption at the bottom said:

Dozens of city employees joined the event for a great cause.

Tired of pacing, Thomas took his seat again.

"Guess that explains how they know each other."

"I don't know. Those emails go back years. This is from May."

He was struggling with the motive—they both were.

"So, what, she's been sleeping with this guy for two years just to swipe some emails? There's got to be better ways to do that, right?"

"No, I don't know. There's something else going on. I just can't figure what it is."

Angela's page came next. Her profile image was casual, a young woman caught midlaugh. Lines creased the corners of her eyes. She was outside, glasses perched on her head, a wicker chair in the background. It was a real moment, the kind of candid scene people tried hard to emulate. Teri opened the album.

"Hmm."

"What?"

The pictures scrolled by, all shots of Angela. Holiday photos with her family joined vacation shots on sunny beaches; a series at the bottom showed her standing between towering pines on a hiking trail.

"Maybe nothing."

"Maybe something. What?"

"No kids."

He scanned the page, looked back.

"So?"

"No boyfriends, no husbands."

"She don't need a man. I don't get it."

"You wouldn't."

"What's that supposed to mean?"

She was about to answer when her phone lit up.

"You gonna answer that?" Thomas said.

The number was local but unfamiliar. She flipped the phone over.

"Not a chance."

"OK." He slid the pad over, pen in hand. "Let's figure this out."

He bent over the page, ready to take down everything.

"You really like lists," she said.

"Helps me stay organized. Sometimes seeing it written down can help."

"Well, from what I can see, these are ledger sheets of some kind. They're tracking money, that's for certain."

"OK."

Her phone chimed, a voice mail waiting. She ignored it.

"She's not doing his taxes, you know, so it has to be some kind of slush fund, or money laundering, something like that. Something shady as shit or he wouldn't be hiding it."

"Agreed." He added her comments to the list. "And we have these emails. Whatever C10 is, that's important."

"Does that sound familiar to you?" she said.

He thought about it, shook his head.

"Not at all."

"OK, well, you follow the money, so I bet you if we find out what that is, we'll find out where the money's going and who's sending it there."

She watched him write. Focused on the list of questions that seemed to never stop coming. Every time they answered one, two more popped up. He chimed in.

"Angela worked downtown, but she has no family, no boyfriends, no significant others that are looking for her right now."

That's why there was no report. She was four days gone and two of those were on the weekend. Reasonable suspicion would start sometime today if she didn't show up for work.

"They will soon."

Thomas looked up.

"Is that good or bad for us?"

She didn't know. Police involvement of the uncrooked kind would be more than welcome, but it was impossible to sort who was who in that capacity. Any more interference from one of Roman's men would be devastating.

"Undecided. I'd rather avoid any run-ins with the APD if we can."

Thomas finished their list of bullets and underlined the bottom with a flourish.

"We know ... not much."

He was right, but she was hopeful.

"We know who she is. Angela Hoffman is a real person, and we know she had a habit of being at the Gardners in the afternoon."

"Listening," he said.

"Like Hayley said, she was there a lot. They were dating or at least involved. I think she came across something, whatever this C10 is, and it went deep. Look at how many people are involved."

"So she stays with him, just to collect evidence?"

"Have you seen how people respond to this guy? They're afraid. Maybe she made a decision"

"Keep your enemies close."

"Something like that."

He chewed it over, drawing tight circles in pen on the page.

"What else makes sense?" she said.

"So, if that's true, why not turn him in?"

"Same reason we can't. No evidence. But look, she's working with this Brian guy. So, someone out there was helping. Someone knows what she knew."

"Think we can find him?"

"We can email him if nothing else."

"That's an encrypted server, you think he'd respond to us?"

"Not sure, but let's start a little closer to home."

Teri opened her phone and typed out a message to Hayley. Maybe she had more information than she knew. Something she'd overheard.

Teri: Did your dad mention anything about C10 or the Central Project?

Quicker than expected, a message came back.

Hayley: No but he works on a lot of city stuff. Boards and things. Sorry.

"OK, maybe it's something with city planning. That would make sense, right?"

She typed back: Thanks.

"There'd be news coverage at least," Thomas said.

"If we knew what it was called. This sounds like some kind of code."

She entered "Central Project Asheville" in the search engine and hit Enter. Nothing returned mentioning plans or ongoing improvements downtown. She tried again with "Biltmore" and "City Council." Same result. When she entered "Roman Gardner" and "Central Project," she got a news article from two years ago that mentioned plans to revitalize a park downtown with the city planning authority. Short of a large grant donation for the cause, there was nothing suspicious or relevant.

"We're getting nowhere," she said.

"Try Brian, see what we can dig up on him."

She entered the name in the search. No exact matches returned. She narrowed the search with the usual keywords, same result.

"Doesn't exist," she said.

"Alias?"

"Maybe."

She tried different spellings, variations on the last name. Nothing solid.

"Unless he's a German soccer player, I got nothing."

"Try the email," he said.

She typed the email, hoping it would come up attached to something. A PDF, a contact page. It brought up the SpryteMail home page but nothing else.

He pointed to the screen.

"If they're using this server, they don't want to be tracked, so this isn't official channels and this guy Brian either doesn't exist or he's using a fake name."

"Wouldn't you come up with a better name?"

He shrugged.

"She used her real name. I think this is someone she trusts, but he's real good at not being found."

"A backup plan maybe? If something happens to her, this guy takes it public?"

"Maybe, but then, where is he?"

It was a dead end.

She stood and walked to the bed, fighting the urge to sleep for the rest of the day. Another half an Addie would keep her going. She popped the pill and lay back.

"Let's send him a message," Thomas said.

"Brian?"

"Yeah. We'll say we're friends. Mutual interests. See what he knows."

"Would you respond to a random message from an unknown account?"

"Maybe, maybe not. Depends on the situation. We don't know what his is."

She thought it over.

"Are we friends? Maybe he's part of this."

"We should try. Set up a new account, see if he answers."

"Alright, I'm in, but don't mention the murder. Let him lead."

She lay on the bed, fighting off sleep while the pill kicked in. Thomas tapped away at the keyboard. The clicking keys were soothing while she rested, let this new information sink in. Hayley had handed them everything they needed; it just had to be decoded. This was their break, it had to be.

"There. Sent," he said with a final decisive tap. "Now we wait and see if he responds."

"He won't," she said.

"Way to be positive," Thomas said, and frowned at her. He took up his normal spot on the couch. Phone out. She wanted to say she was positive he wouldn't respond but decided against it.

He was already hard at work. She felt guilty not helping but fatigue had taken its toll.

"I'm going to look for more on this project. We're missing something," he said.

"I'm just gonna lay here for a few minutes. Close my eyes."

At some point her phone buzzed. When she looked up again, Thomas was still on the couch, shoes off. Her head was fuzzy and muscles stiff when she sat up.

"How long was I out?"

"Hour and a half ... two maybe."

She barely remembered closing her eyes.

"What I miss?"

"Not a thing. Your phone's blinking."

She picked up the device, one missed message.

The text was from Hayley, simple.

```
Hayley: He knows.
```

Ch. 22

The coffee was hot; that was the only thing good about it. The fact that it tasted like reheated grounds from three days ago was tempered by bigger concerns hanging between them at the small dining room table downstairs. Breakfast ran until ten and they both sat in front of plates of buffet items, waiting out the last half hour. Thomas stabbed at too-yellow scrambled eggs while she watched his eyes. They were puffier than usual. He looked drawn. She had never seen him this tired. They were both deteriorating even if he was going at a slower pace.

The message had been clear. He knew. Somehow Roman figured out his daughter had snuck out and met with them. No amount of discussion could change those words. All night they had gone over options until they ran out of words. When they gave up, Teri curled in the bed, terrified that she had made things worse. First, Thomas had been drawn in because of her impulsive actions, but now Hayley was in danger too. What would Roman do to his own daughter?

Her bag was packed. They knew they had to move, even if it wasn't clear where. Uncomfortable, ashamed, she pulled up the messages from yesterday.

```
Hayley: He knows.
Teri: He knows what?
Hayley: Somehow, he just knows. He's acting
different. I think I was followed.
Teri: Maybe you're paranoid?
Hayley: You don't know him. He's angry. He
hasn't said a word since I got home.
Teri: Is that unusual?
Hayley: Only if I'm what he's mad about.
Teri: Are you safe, do you have somewhere to
go?
Hayley: I'll be fine.
```

The final message, ominous, cut through her walls, sent a chill to her core.

```
Hayley: He'll find you.
```

The silence was too much.

"We're in trouble, aren't we?" she said.

He set the fork down, done pretending he wanted any of it.

"It's not good. We can't keep running."

"I'm sorry, I know this is my fault."

His face turned to a frown.

"What would you do different?"

She shifted, uncomfortable.

"Name one thing you would do different if you had the chance."

"I would have told you I was going yesterday."

"And I would have gone with you. No difference."

"But if you talked me out of it—"

"We still wouldn't know anything. This isn't your fault. This is Roman, remember that."

"OK."

"So, let's skip apologies for now. Let's get ourselves unfucked first."

She nodded, pushed the plate away.

"Alright."

The room was cold, conditioned air blasting down from above. They were at the only free table, and they were both tired of the room. Conversation at other tables was sporadic and uninteresting. Done eating, she dedicated herself to finishing the mediocre coffee so they could escape the cramped confines with its undersized furniture. To the left a woman coughed, snorted and coughed again. Mouth uncovered, phlegm rocketed through the air and landed on two plates of waffles, eggs and a blueberry muffin.

"Any response from Brian?" she said.

Thomas had been watching the mail server on his phone all morning.

"Nothing yet."

She wanted to say it, that he was too safe to take a risk on them but decided to let hope survive.

"I was thinking about plan B," she said.

"There's a plan B?"

"We know who Angela is. Maybe we can find out where she lived."

"Breaking and entering twice in one week?"

"Just entering. We'll try not to break anything. It's the only idea I have."

"It's the only thing we've got left, I think," he said.

Another family entered the dining room, two small kids, one with a runny nose.

"I'm going to the room," she said. "Let's get out of here."

"Right behind you. You want me to bring you a coffee?"

She smirked over her shoulder.

"Yeah. Let me know if you find some."

She tossed the Styrofoam cup in the trash on her way out.

The call came as she was passing through the lobby on the way to the elevators. Same number as before. She stared at the caller display, hit Ignore and slid the phone in her pocket. A young couple stepped out when the doors opened; bags in hand, they skirted her on their way to the lobby. As she stepped on, the phone dinged. Another message. Alone in the car, she retrieved the phone, hit the voice mail button.

"Mrs. Fletcher. Detective Pastore with Asheville Police Department. If you have a minute, I'd like to talk to you. I think you may be able to help us with a difficult case. Thanks."

The man read out his number and hung up.

He sounded weird. More distant than the last time they spoke. More important, how had he found her? Rubbing the phone, she watched the elevator numbers climb to three. Before it stopped, she hit Call Back.

"Pastore."

"How'd you get my number?"

A short pause. Then back on top.

"Who am I speaking with?"

"You tell me."

The phone rustled; he was checking.

"Mrs. Fletcher. Great to hear from you. I wanted to ask some questions, if you have a minute."

She held the door, choosing the seclusion of the elevator for now.

"Haven't answered mine yet."

"Your number? Well, you called 911 last"—he checked the notes— "Thursday night, around five p.m., is that right?"

He didn't know who she was.

"I did," she said, and stepped into the hall.

"It was a mistake."

He rustled some papers. She could hear an old chair creak in the background.

"Are you sure?"

"Sure that I made a mistake? Yeah, the officer made that pretty clear."

He didn't answer that. She moved down the hall, listening as he sorted through notes.

"The responding officer was ... Wallace and Moreno?"

"The first one."

She had to give him credit on his instincts. Something about the name must have clicked, because his tone changed in an instant.

"Have we spoken before?" he said.

"Tell me," she said.

She paused, fished for the key card with her free hand, cradling the phone on her shoulder.

"I'm guessing you have something to do with Officer Wallace's recent accident."

"I hope so," she said, knowing it was dumb, not caring. The hatred for that man boiled up in seconds.

"Are you home?"

"No, and don't bother. There's nothing there anymore."

She slid the card in the door, the light changing. She stopped short, fingers resting on the handle. Was that a cough? It could have been on the phone.

"Mrs. Fletcher, I need to talk to you. We can help each other out."

"Call you back," she said, and hit End.

Easing back, she typed out a message as quick as possible.

`Teri: Gt uot now.`

Bedsprings creaked. A heavy weight coming off the mattress. She ran.

There were three doors to clear between her and the stairs. Five the other way. She hit the exit door at the same time one of the rooms opened. If it was hers, the unwelcome visitor wouldn't be far behind. It was too far to run. She had to move faster than she ever had. Too little time to think. She placed a foot sideways on the runner for the stairs, grabbed the rail.

"This is a terrible idea."

It was. She let go and slid down the runner on the side of her foot, reaching the bottom in seconds. Unable to stop, she flew off the end, hit the wall and bounced back. The next rail waited, stopping her fall as her hand grasped the painted metal. Getting in position, she was down the next flight just as fast, stopping short of the end this time. She wasn't sure if anyone followed, but she wasn't giving them time to catch up. Down two flights, barreling down the third, she was a couple feet from the final landing when her throat hitched. Her collar closed tight around her neck and her feet shot out from under her. Landing hard on her ass for the second time this week. The sharp angle of a stair dug into her side. She tried to cry out but choked on it.

A woman's voice shouted, amplified in the open space.

"Don't move. Sit still."

Teri grasped at gloved fingers that had her by the shirt. Strong hands had her off the steps and on her face in seconds.

"Hold still. I mean it."

With the choke released, she went into a coughing fit, spitting snot and saliva on the concrete. The woman waited until she stopped, something hard pressed to her spine.

"You Teri?"

She couldn't respond, choked again.

"Are you Teri Fletcher?"

She shook her head.

The woman eased up, holding her to the floor.

"You got ID?"

She shook her head again, trying to find words.

"No ... upstairs."

Her wallet was in the backpack, on the bed. She had nothing to identify her.

"Why were you running?"

Teri dissolved into a fit of coughs again. Maybe she played it up, went for sympathy. It worked.

The woman removed the sharp object digging into her back. She stepped back, letting her up. Teri turned over, pulled herself up on the stairs. The woman, with a hand at her side, ready to draw, was the one she'd seen last at the apartment door. Wallace's partner.

"I know you?" she said.

Letting her head fall forward, Teri kept her face down. Shook her head. This must be Moreno and if she was here, that meant Wallace was upstairs. It was an ambush. She hoped Thomas had gotten the message, gotten out in time.

Hand rubbing her throat, she glanced up at intervals, watching the woman's movements.

"Why were you running?" she said again.

"Saw a ghost," Teri said before coughing again.

"I want you to hold still till my partner comes, you hear me?"

She rocked her head, no plans on moving. The woman spoke into her radio.

"Mark, come in."

It was robotic, broken with static, but she recognized the voice that responded.

"Go ahead."

"Give me a description on the suspect."

The answer that came was clear, no doubt that it was her. Everything but the birthmark on her right leg.

"Suspect detained in the west stairwell. Awaiting backup."

"Ten-four. En route."

Teri gasped, trying to will her voice box to work.

"Tried ... to ... ill me," she managed.

She struggled to say more.

"Shut up. Just sit there. You're being detained for suspicion of trafficking narcotics. Say yes if you understand."

Teri shook her head. "What?"

"Are you Teri Fletcher?"

She nodded.

"You ... don't ..." It hurt to speak. She swallowed. Her throat was bruised and swollen.

"You don't understand," she said.

"Don't speak unless you're answering questions. Give me lip and I'm putting the cuffs on, understand?" Moreno's foot kicked out and pushed away the cane that had rattled across the floor when she landed.

Teri gave up. It was too difficult to form coherent words, and this woman wouldn't understand anyway. She was doing her job, apprehending a drug dealer. Teri glanced at the cane, too far away. The woman read her mind.

"Don't. The only reason you're not facedown right now is you being ... disabled." She had to search for a word that wasn't too offensive.

"Don't make me regret that."

Teri decided right then to find a way to make her regret that.

Time passed, but Officer Wallace never appeared. Moreno called for a status report.

"I've got the other one—he's on foot. Bring the girl to the car. I'll meet you there."

She frowned. Officer Moreno didn't want to deal with this situation alone.

"On your feet."

"I can't," she said.

"Get up or I'll get you up."

"Then get me up. I can't move." She flexed her legs to prove the point.

"It's kind of a bitch, but they don't just work on command anymore."

"If you're faking, you won't be walking anywhere for a week."

"Your compassion is overwhelming. Just let me rest a minute."

The woman snapped the holster on her weapon, securing it, and snaked an arm under Teri's shoulder.

"Come on, no time for this shit."

The uppercut that came next was unexpected, the crunch of the poor cop's teeth proof that everyone underestimated what she could do if her legs weren't involved. Blood gushed from the woman's mouth, making Teri certain she had bitten her tongue or had one of those pearly whites knocked loose. Moreno tried to say "You bitch," but it came out garbled through spit and red bubbles.

Just enough to get her wind back, the rest time had given Teri the upper hand, aided by surprise. She figured that was it. Luck was done saving her ass. If she got to the door, it would be a miracle, and if she got outside, nothing short of divine intervention, but when she burst through the exit, stumbled forward and landed face-first in the grass, the woman wasn't behind her. The steel door slammed shut and stayed that way. The Camry was gone, the space under their tree empty. She had to hide, fast.

A walled-in area about eight feet across waited a few yards away up a short hill. On hands and knees, she scrambled, got going and worked her way over the hump to a wood gate across a wide entrance. The rank odor was immediate, a punch to the chest when she slid inside. A rusted green dumpster swarming with flies squatted in the space with inches on either side.

The stench was overpowering even as she held her breath and pushed into the tight space. Abrasive stone opened scratches on her back and arms. Putrid, rotten garbage did battle with a gag reflex that was losing fast. Pressed tight against the wall, she couldn't breathe deep enough to choke on the foul odor or retch even if she wanted to. If the police woman dared to follow, the gun belt and vest would never make it through. They'd have to take the dumpster out. Turning the corner at the back of the enclosure, she decided that's what they would have to do; nothing was getting her out once she was wedged in.

Arms pinned at chest level, body secure behind the once green, metal behemoth, her stomach lurched at the rancid smell of spoiled milk and what was either rotten fruit or human feces. It made her mouth fill with saliva, her guts clench, but she managed to hold it in. *Another great idea.*

When she had settled that it couldn't get worse, a skitter of miniature, hair like feet crossed her ankle; she yelped but forced herself to contain the sound. She kicked, hoping to knock the tiny creature off. It didn't work, turning the other way it ran up her calf, inside her pants leg. She screamed into closed teeth. The creature ran around her leg, about faced and scurried off, leaving her with balled fists and skin crawling all over. Forcing herself to remain calm took all her remaining willpower. On the bright side, no one had come yet, no booming voice demanded her surrender, anxious to take revenge for a cheap shot. She allowed herself to think it wasn't coming.

The metal door slammed open, killing that hope. Footsteps echoed on concrete, radio chatter too distorted to make out. Pinned like a rat in a corner, she listened, sweat running into her eye, forcing it closed. Nearer now, at the bottom of the hill. She sounded funny, scuffing the pavement as she went. Her steps irregular.

Go away, go away, go away, Teri chanted.

Every scenario she envisioned involved handcuffs and her face in the smelly, garbage-soaked ground. There had been time—she hadn't known that, but if she had run, there had been time. She could be far away by now. It was a wish, hindsight at its best. She could barely walk; running was out of the question. She would have collapsed on the road in plain view. Waiting to be picked up. Making it easy for them.

The footsteps continued but never came closer. Surrounded by echo and insulated by concrete, it sounded like she was stumbling, not looking for a suspect. Moreno either didn't know where to look or she wasn't trying to. The hiding space was too obvious, why wasn't she coming?

The radio cracked, that familiar voice.

"Lost him ..." Something garbled. "Coming back."

The response was slurred, unintelligible.

"You alright Moreno?"

"Fine. Fyuck ith. Going outh front."

Footsteps retreated; the heavy door opened, then shut. She waited, gagged, spit to the side. They never came back. She was alone, her and the roaches.

The phone was still in her pocket. Reaching down, she pulled it free, managed to raise it to eye level. She punched in Thomas's number and hit Call. He answered on the first ring.

"Where are you?" He spoke fast, rattled.

"You could say I'm between a rock and an awful place. How did you get away?"

"I lost him a while back, but that won't last forever. Can you get to the road behind the hotel?"

"Yeah."

"OK, follow that. Don't stand still. They're looking for us now. Get to Wedgefield. I'll pick you up."

She looked forward to getting away from this smell as soon as possible, but Wedgefield was a neighborhood over. It would be difficult to do at all and impossible unnoticed.

"Should I go now?"

"Go now. I'll be there in a few minutes."

"Keep your eyes open," she said.

'Just hurry.'

Ch. 23

A trail of blood formed a Pollock on the sidewalk. Free of
the rank confines, she hobbled to the sidewalk outside the
exit door. The spots were a wandering drunk's path to
nowhere. The punch must have been good, knocking Moreno
this far off center. Her cane was inside, but it was too much to
risk. It was now a casualty of survival. From here out, she'd
have to do her best without it. Up a short incline, she came out
on a raised two-lane behind the hotel.

An access road to a smattering of homes on the ridge, no
cars in sight. The road dead-ended at a side lot off a one-story
home, with an empty driveway and a close grove of trees along
the boundary. A quarter mile of empty two-lane to the back
and dark windows were all the motivation she needed to cross
a short stretch of lawn into the cover of untended woodland.

Wedgefield, a small subdivision of working-class homes, would be about five hundred feet through the grove, according to Google Maps. The terrain was steep, running downhill in a ravine and then turning up again. The down she handled well, sitting where necessary, working over fallen branches. On the way up, a broken limb snapped short served as a walking stick to get over the hardest part. It was slow going but she was proud of herself for making progress.

Decades of pine needles and discarded trash littered the ground, making the incline a treacherous path to take. A half-buried tire turned into a convenient handhold to pull herself up and out of the ravine. On flat land, she emerged behind a row of houses that made up the back side of Wedgefield. This lot looked like it hadn't been used for anything more than drinking beer and tossing fast-food wrappers.

Through layers of irregularly spaced trunks, she saw cluttered backyards, an above ground pool, green with algae, and most of a rotted privacy fence that blocked her progress to the road. To the right, a clearing followed the contour of the hills that became the mountains outside of Asheville.

Her overgrown lot between the two narrowed as it climbed the opposing hill, squeezed between irregular property lines that dwindled the tree cover to nothing. At the point, a row of rusted cars sat beyond a neglected chain-link fence, twisted and sagging with age. Overgrown and broken down, a section of rusted chain link leaned against the low side of a ditch with barely enough give to slip through.

The makeshift gate dropped her out in the front parking lot of a massive junkyard. Stepping from the shadows, she found herself surrounded by rusted fenders and truck beds like remnants of a forgotten war. Across thirty feet of gravel, a corroded metal gate hung open. Beyond that, Wedgefield Drive and, she hoped, Thomas waited for her to come out.

Without extra support, she would have to move quick and try not to be seen. The walking stick that had gotten her this far was lost somewhere behind. To the right, a metal shed large enough to house several small planes had only one open bay and shadow beyond. She felt confident.

Halfway across, a booming voice destroyed that. It cut the still air in two with its aggressive timbre. The accent was deep, Appalachia throughout. He had twice the distance she had to clear before he was a threat, but even without a body he was still intimidating.

"Hey, what you doin' down there?"

She picked up speed, moving across uneven rock. Her feet, slipping in the gravel, went sideways, so that she stumbled more than she ran.

This time the shout was louder as a heavy man, with shaved head and massive unruly beard, appeared.

"You can't be over there. Come back here."

The man made a move to come after her, but she didn't know how far he got. Head low, she went straight for the gate, taking an angle that guaranteed she'd make it first. He came behind in a trot, gravel crunching under work boots. She didn't have time to fear what would happen when he caught her. The Camry appeared like a guardian angel from nowhere. It had pulled out of a side road cloaked in overgrowth and came to a stop outside the gate. Seeing the car, the man chose to stop chasing and shout again.

"You stay out of there or I'm callin' the cops. You hear me?" Then lower: "Stupid kids."

When the car stopped, she hopped in without a word. Thomas backed out of the gravel drive and swung around in a swift motion.

"Good timing."

"Lucky I saw you. What the hell were you doing in there?"

"Taking the scenic route."

She pulled an errant pine needle from her hair as they passed through the simple lots and came to a dead end at a dirt path that would be a stretch to call a road.

"Hang on," he said.

The car whipped out on the dirt, slid on the loose surface and came back. They rocked and lurched over a pothole-filled section that connected Wedgefield to a collection of country roads. When the car stopped bouncing, tires found smooth asphalt and they picked up speed away from the highway and developed property.

"Where are we going?" she said.

"No idea. I barely got away from that guy. Had to drive through a construction zone. Surprised it worked, to tell you the truth."

"If they're coming after us in uniform, they're gonna be looking for this car."

"I know. We have to get off the roads. Any ideas?"

She had none. None that were helpful. Driving straight through Roman's front door seemed like a good idea.

"How did they find us?"

She didn't have that answer either.

"They followed her, that's all I can figure. But they could have come last night. Why wait?"

There were too many unanswered questions. As they reached a dead end, Thomas cranked the wheel and headed a new way. All roads looked the same on this side of the city, flanked by warehouses, trees and the occasional single story set back from the road. She looked at her phone, pulled up Maps to find their location.

"Pull off here," she said, indicating a gravel lot with a plain metal shed. The sign said MILLER METAL WORKS, and the lot was empty. The car rolled to a stop in a cloud of dust. Prepared, Thomas turned them around, pointing the nose toward the road for a quick getaway. He kept his eyes on the road, a lookout watching for squad cars. If they didn't outrun the cops, she knew he would give it everything he had.

"I've got an idea. Turn off your phone."

Without question he held down the power button on his own phone while she scrolled through pages on hers, looking for something that might not exist. The signal was weak, pages buffered for minutes before loading. It blinked a red battery, uncharged overnight. Every car that passed was their ticket to jail.

"What are you looking for?"

"This," she said, and clicked a link. The page that loaded had an address that she copied and pasted into Maps. With the directions on-screen, she memorized the route, double-checked and turned off her phone too.

"OK, go that way," she said, pointing to the right.

"You think they tracked our phones?"

"All it takes is a warrant, right?"

"I don't know honestly."

"Let's be safe. Better to be off the grid now. If they didn't think of it already, they will."

He pulled out, took a right and sped up as fast as they could go without drawing attention. She felt his desire to floor it, to push the engine to its limit. It was in the air and she wanted it too.

"Where are we going?" he asked.

"Take a left at the intersection."

The Camry slowed, took the turn and revved again.

"Angela Hoffman's house. I'm out of ideas otherwise."

He gave no sign of disapproval.

"Tell me where to go."

A brick house at the bottom of a sloping hill, Angela's home was shrouded in large shade trees that dominated the front lawn. In the back, a stand of pine extended to a wood

privacy fence, in much better condition than the ones in
Wedgefield. She directed him past the house and down the
street to a turnaround half a block away. They came to a stop
under the shade of a large oak. Thomas turned the car so the
license plate was hidden from the road. The sun was high in
the sky; except for the shadows where they parked, the street
was bright. A lawn mower hummed somewhere.

They hadn't noticed any other cars on first pass, though
both were looking. Teri noticed the home was deserted, several
days of mail in a metal box on the porch. Like other homes on
the street, it was quiet, waiting for its owner to return. Only
this one had been waiting longer and she was never coming
back.

Doing their best to look natural, they crept along the
shoulder, a couple out for a walk if any neighbors happened to
be watching through parted blinds.

The quickest and safest bet, they crossed the backyard,
which had been recently cut. She knew they stood
abetter chance of going unnoticed if they acted like they
belonged there. So they took a direct path across the
lawn to a flagstone walkway and open garage. The garage
gave them a safe place to plan their way in.

"That was easy," Thomas said.

"So far."

Ch. 24

A screen and a four-paned wood panel door stood between them and the answers they needed.

"How do we get in?"

Teri walked out to the drive, where rows of flagstones had been arranged in succession, creating a Better Homes and Gardens feel. She hefted one of the cement stones—five pounds, maybe ten—and hauled it back to the garage.

"Try this," she said, and handed over the stone.

"No sense sneaking around. It's not like she's coming home."

"What about an alarm?"

"Risk it," she said.

There was no alarm. Wrapped in a towel from a bucket in the garage, the stone shattered the window with almost no sound. Short of a few jagged edges and a pile of glass on the inside, entry was easy.

"You get the cake job," she said.

Now inside, it was even quieter. All the rooms were dark, from the pantry at the back door, through the kitchen and to the living room beyond, which was visible in one shot. A stale thick odor signaled that no one had stirred the atmosphere recently. Faint perfume lingered. Still cautious after the abrupt entrance, they spoke in hushed tones.

"Where do you want to start?" he said.

"I don't know—look everywhere. I'm not even sure what to look for."

They moved through the kitchen, each step an announcement to any predator that waited motionless beyond. As their eyes adjusted, she made note of everything in sight. The counters were empty, clean. A coffee cup with a lipstick stain was the only item out of place.

"Look for a laptop, printouts, stuff like that. Anything with information on it."

"Will it help?"

She rounded on him, hissing in a whisper.

"I'm grasping at straws. Would you just go with it?"

He went with it, moving toward a hall that extended from the main rooms of the house.

"It's strange," he said.

"What?"

"No one's been here. It's completely untouched."

"What's your point? No one knows she's missing, remember?"

"Roman knows."

She thought about that. It *was* strange that Angela's home hadn't been raided the way hers had. It gnawed at her while Thomas disappeared down the hall.

Curtains pulled, the windows were still covered from the last morning Angela lived here. It was dark and several degrees cooler in the living room, where Teri poked at the ash in a stone fireplace. She allowed herself to believe the temperature was the reason her arm hairs stood on end as she passed through by a well-worn rolled armchair and a decorative love seat. A magazine lay face down on the end table between them. The front door was still locked, the dead bolt open. A white box beside the doorframe got her attention.

"Hey, check this out."

Thomas came up behind her, looking over her shoulder at a blank LCD screen.

"It's disconnected," she said.

"I guess they took a soft touch on this one."

She reached for the knob, changed her mind and rubbed her hand on her pants. Best not to leave fingerprints. Things were not what they seemed.

"Explains what I found, though."

"What did you find?" she said.

He motioned for her to follow, and they walked down the hall to an open door on the left. Once inside, he stood in front of closet doors that had been left open as well.

"Take a look."

At first glance it looked normal, except for a shoe box that had been left out on the floor.

"What am I missing?" she said.

"You don't see it. What was in the box?"

Teri examined the scene looking for something unusual.

"By looking at it, I'd guess shoes."

"No, look at these." He pointed a row of similar boxes in the closet. "These are new. This box is ratty, old like the kind you put photos in."

"Or papers, like emails."

"Now you see it. Someone just tossed it aside when they got what they wanted."

"You think someone cleaned the place?"

"It's possible, right?"

It was possible, even plausible.

"What other rooms have you checked?"

"Just this one and the bathroom. Nothing unusual. Some clothes on the floor, makeup on the sink."

Back in the hall, she continued searching. The bathroom was on the opposite side, but there was another room on their wall before the bedroom. One they had passed by. She went in. As guessed, it was an office. A large wood desk, highly polished, sat against the wall. A plush leather office chair that put hers to shame waited behind it. On the desk, a stack of papers with a crystal weight on top joined a handful of pens, a legal pad and a desk calendar. Nothing unusual.

The chair absorbed her weight as she sank into it. It swiveled with ease, no resistance. Both hands on the desk, she waited for Thomas to enter.

"Find anything?"

"No, but that's the point, isn't it?"

"What did they take?"

She blew at a dust line on the desk surface.

"The keyboard is gone."

She opened doors on the sides of the desk until she found an empty cavity on the left.

"Tower's gone, cables and all."

"So they took the whole thing. Nothing left behind."

"Clean," she said.

She pushed away from the desk and stood. Whoever did this was precise. If you weren't looking for a problem, you wouldn't find one. At least until you found the busted windowpane.

"We helped them. Now even if someone makes a fuss, it looks like a robbery."

"Great." He left her alone in the room.

She found him in the living room, examining a picture of Angela and an older couple that could have been her parents. She was younger, early twenties maybe. The man and woman on each side were shorter than she was by several inches.

For the second time Teri studied the room. The decor was spare for a woman in her thirties. There was no TV. A coffee table in the middle of the space supported a broad-leaf houseplant wilting around the edges in front of the love seat with a throw across the back. The walls were blank except for a pair of matching framed prints. A beautiful woman in a flowing skirt, posed mid-dance, a red rose in her shimmering black hair.

Nothing was out of place, no signs of forced entry. The room was immaculate from carefully arranged mantelpiece to freshly cleaned rug. This kind of attention took dedication; Angela was not a going-out, coming-home-late type.

Next to the magazine was a coaster with a stain on it, maybe wine, and a pull-chain lamp. She spent a lot of time there.

"This place is empty. What are we looking for?"

That question was getting harder to answer. It appeared Roman had beat them to it.

"Let's hope we know it when we see it."

Sitting on the edge of the chair she hoped to see things from Angela's point of view. The magazine was curled, well read. She picked it up. Underneath, a slim black tablet rested.

"Like that?" he said.

"Exactly like that," she said.

The battery was good with a thin black wire stretching to an outlet it shared with the lamp. It was an e-reader, but it had Internet and apps as well. Pulling up the browser, she went straight to Internet history.

"Let's see what she's been looking up."

The site list was average: shopping, weather, a handful of government links. She clicked the last one, receiving a search box and a list of current hearings. None of the entries were familiar. When she clicked one, a pop-up asked for a username and password. She closed the link.

"Do we have something?" Thomas leaned in, watching her work.

"Not yet, hold on."

Farther down the history, she found an article and clicked that. The headline read:

<u>Downtown Demolition Drags On—Hearing Draws Close</u>
She skimmed the article, while a grin tugged at her mouth.
"Now here's something."

Thomas edged in, reading over her shoulder.

The demolition project for the Carrier X revitalization program that would install a new community outreach center downtown has hit another hurdle. Key funders are tied up in red tape over legal issues pertaining to how land was obtained for the project and specifically questions about how efforts to ensure the safe removal of potentially hazardous materials at the site were handled.

Earlier this year it was discovered that a team of officials had potentially falsified reports about the mishandling of chemicals labeled as a biological threat to the local ecosystem. Carrier, when reached for comment, stated, "There is no evidence to support these claims and the accusation is preposterous." While the court handles the case, Carrier is losing money for every day the project goes unfinished, a liability they are seeking damages for in a countersuit. It's worth noting that a related case, alleging misconduct in purchasing the property that would become the new outreach center, is taking place in criminal court. The Carrier company is being sued for misrepresenting intentions when the block of land being developed was purchased three years prior and for failing to submit proper paperwork prior to breaking ground.

A spokesman for the company stated, "All forms were submitted and verified. Their disappearance amounts to a clerical issue, nothing more."

As the process drags on, it's becoming unclear when or if the project will resume. While the property remains unused, pressure to sell mounts from representatives seeking a commercial addition in the area, which serves as a prime retail location with cross traffic from Patton, Haywood and nearby I-26.

She moved to the couch. Thomas took a spot next to her, the tablet on the coffee table.

"That *is* interesting."

"Maybe this is the project. This might be the C10."

He mulled over the article.

"Where have I seen Carrier signs? Haven't you seen those somewhere?"

It clicked.

"I have, on Patton. At the bottom of the hill, right before the highway. There's a bus stop or something where those homeless people are."

"It's a mission," Thomas said. "They have a shelter and soup kitchen down there. They've been talking about expanding for years."

"Right, so this thing they're building, it must be there. That's why it's been roped off for like …"

"Ever?"

"Yeah. So, what's Roman got to do with an outreach center downtown?"

She stood up, walked to the kitchen, using the wall for support.

"Well, he's taking money, right?"

"Like a bribe," he said.

"Exactly, so … there's only two reasons either to help push this project through …"

She let him finish the sentence.

"Or to stop it."

He started tapping the screen, clicking through related articles.

"My money is on stop it. It sounds like someone, or in this case maybe a lot of someones, don't want that center built," she said.

"Why would they? Wouldn't it be more valuable as a restaurant or a club or something?"

"Probably, and attract a more profitable crowd too, right? So someone … or more than one want it shut down. They string up a bunch of red tape and …"

Thomas tapped on the tablet, focused on a block of text that flew by with the flick of a finger. He stopped it with a touch.

"And … guess who is representing the Carrier company against the charges of misconduct?"

"Roman?"

"His firm is. Says it right here."

She took the tablet and read the article. It said that Welch, Lawson & Gardner was acting on behalf of Carrier in the case.

"That doesn't make sense. He's defending them."

"Unless he isn't."

"Unless he's sabotaging the case."

"Exactly."

Teri laughed.

"Gut your own case—in exchange you gain the favor of a bunch of elite during your bid for judgeship. Sound about evil enough?"

"Sounds like our guy to me."

She fell onto the couch.

"So, our guy is a garden-variety greedy asshole and a murderer," she said. "We can stop him. He's nothing special."

"With a body," he said.

Thomas looked up from the screen, doubt working its way in.

"I've got an idea," she said. "Move over."

She laid the tablet on the table and opened the email app. Hopefully Angela was an Android fan. The tablet opened a Gmail account.

"Perfect. This might work. She's logged into Gmail, which means ..."

Thomas watched while she moved through screens too fast to follow. She talked out loud, narrating her actions. Under Apps, she opened Maps and hit the menu. She tapped through the menu, and a map of the neighborhood they were in appeared, covered in little red dots.

"Bingo!"

"What? Are those like trackers?"

"That's exactly what they are. People don't realize your history tracks across all devices. Everything is cloud these days. Maps keep a record of everywhere your phone pings, every hour ... every day. This is everywhere Angela went this month. So, if I pull up last Thursday ..."

She changed the date to last week, the day Angela died.

"This is her day and we can track it by the hour." She hit a button to show a timeline of events.

"You've got to be kidding," she said.

Thomas leaned over. "No way."

On-screen a blue line connected dots from where they were sitting, downtown, out for lunch around noon and then to Roman's neighborhood. Shortly after that, the phone pinged only a few blocks away, about ten feet onshore at Lake Julian.

"It's the plant," she said.

"How's that possible?"

"I don't know, but it fits. He'd want her close, where he could keep an eye on her."

The dot was the outer edge of a clearing that sat apart from the main body of the industrial plant.

"Let's go," he said.

Ch. 25

Teri watched the leaves make shadows dance on the window while Thomas strapped on his seat belt. Light faded, blending the shadows with darkness, when the sun passed behind a cloud. Soon, the limbs that formed the alcove above would struggle to maintain the leaves that would light themselves on fire and fall to the earth. They were embraced by the darkness, death and the inevitable turn of the seasons. It all made sense, but it didn't.

"You all right?" he asked, hand on the ignition.

"I wish I didn't get it. That this didn't make sense, but it does. She died for nothing. I was hoping maybe … it was something. Maybe she was making a difference, but in the end all she was is another casualty to rich assholes who want to destroy more innocent people to make more money."

She wiped a tear from her eye.

He was going to pay. How wasn't clear but she knew
there was no way he'd get away with it if she still had life in her.

"How the fuck is this the world we live in?"
Unprepared, Thomas offered no response. He watched the
quiet neighborhood through the dirty windshield.

"Forget it," she said. "Let's go find her so we can make this
asshole suffer."

The drive over was slow, taking back roads that switched
back, doubled over themselves. So close, they couldn't
risk blowing cover now. Still early in the afternoon,
Thomas convinced her to hang back, parked off the road
until after the rush. When neither one could stand it any
longer, he cranked up the engine and pointed toward the
Shores.

Winding through neighborhoods, he put them out a
block from the lake and spitting distance from an iron
gate that prevented access to the deserted driveway of an
abandoned plant.

"Now we know," he said, pulling up to the rusted arm
with a weathered sign that read NO TRESPASSING and
VIOLATORS WILL BE PROSECUTED. She waited while he got
out to check for options. If necessary, ramming it was
not out of the question. She hoped he felt the same.

Their opportunity to play Smokey and the
Bandit disappeared when he held up the rusted metal chain
that had been wrapped through metal tubing and around a
pole that stuck out of the ground in a cement base. A
battered padlock hung from one link, connected to
nothing. The chain, the heavy-duty kind you got from
hardware stores, the kind you could winch a car from a lake
with, snaked through his fingers, slinked into a pile on the
pavement. He tossed the end into a growth of weeds and
headed back to the car, stopped halfway like a frightened
deer, eyes so wide she could see the whites, frozen in
midstride.

She flipped around, following his dread-filled gaze to four lanes of traffic and a blue and white squad car that sent a chill down her spine.

"Was that a cop?"

He was in the car before the sentence finished. Self-preservation had broken him from the spell and sent him into overdrive.

"City cop. Don't think he saw us. Come on, let's go."

He dropped the car into gear and lurched forward. When they reached the gate, he hit the gas and pushed against it. The engine roared but the rusted gate refused to budge. After a look in the mirror and a second rev of the engine, the bar gave, grinding open with a squeal that was painful, and they pushed through. A metal-on-metal grate followed as the pole scraped down the driver's side.

"That sounds bad," she said, picturing a bright silver streak against the black paint.

"Not important," he said.

He put it in park, got out and went to wrestle the gate back into position. It took several tries and both of their efforts, but it swung back and clinked into its place against the pole. The patrol car never returned and despite her pounding chest, Teri felt a little more at ease once they pulled down the treelined path that had been a main drive at one time. The concrete was broken in places but apparently had been kept up until recent years. A quarter mile down along the lakeside, blue-green water could be seen through frequent breaks in the trees along the right side. To their left the massive plant appeared at the end of a wide paved road. Barricades, set up at some point to funnel traffic, now served only to block their way. The Camry slid off the road to a dirt path and what looked like fresh tire tracks.

"We're destroying tons of evidence," he said.

"If we find her at the end of this road, it won't matter."

The access road was nothing more than a set of dirt tracks along bumpy, uneven terrain. Heavy tree growth crowded from both sides. Untamed weeds whipped at the doors as they pushed forward. The Camry bounced in and out of deep potholes, bottoming out twice. At the end they emerged into a clearing at least an acre wide. Thomas pulled to the middle of the field and stopped. A pile of gravel and scattered stones overgrown with weeds were the only objects in sight. Surrounded by a ring of evergreens, the lake beyond was visible past narrow trunks. It was empty. This close to winter, there weren't many boats or kayaks on the water.

"See anything?"

He shook his head.

"No. Grass is too high. Try the map again."

She pulled out the tablet, holding it like a map. The red dot was accurate within a few feet. That meant Angela was straight ahead, at the edge of the tree line. She got out, wielding the tablet like a homing device.

"This way," she said, and led a path through knee-high weeds, a straight line of pressed grass in her wake. On top of the location in the map, she turned in circles.

"It's right here," she said.

Behind her, Thomas brushed aside weeds and dug through undergrowth.

"I don't see anything. Wouldn't it … you know, smell?"

It was an incredibly callous thing to say, but he was right. There was no smell. She had always heard dead bodies had a very specific and obvious odor. Even if Angela had been dragged away by a wild animal or something, there was nothing here. No sign there ever had been.

"Look deeper," she said.

Kicking brush with their feet, they pushed past the trees and into the loose soil and rocky shore of the lake. Briars clung in groups, impeding progress, but it was obvious nothing like what they were looking for was out here. It didn't make sense; what could it mean?

"So, what happened to her?" he said.

She shrugged, mouth open.

"I don't know. I mean, it's close—with the time he had, even the walk back would be a tight window. There's nowhere else he could have gone and be here."

"And we're sure he was here?"

"She was."

"Her phone was," he said.

She considered the point.

"Still, he had to bring it here. Why would he do that and not bring the body? If he did … where is she?"

"I don't know either, but it's not here. That's for certain."

She consulted the tablet, the red dot dead center with their location. She verified it against landmarks, putting them right on mark.

"She's here. Spread out."

"I think you're missing something," he said. "Where's the car?"

She held up her hands in frustration.

"I don't know. Now help me look."

In a grid, like a search team they worked the field, arm's length apart so they wouldn't miss anything. The terrain was difficult, especially without the extra support of her now lost cane, but determination carried her through. Every time she slipped, lost her balance, she played it off to a hole in the ground and kept going.

"OK, maybe he took the car after. So, he comes out here, he dumps the body and he takes her car somewhere else, a junkyard or a gravel pit or something."

"No time," she said, and slapped at a briar on her leg. Knocked off-balance, she reached out for support. Thomas grabbed her and helped her up. It was getting late. Soon it would be dark and she doubted their ability to conduct a search at night.

"So, what if he left it here?"

Thomas stopped, prompting her to look back at him. He was focused on the tree line.

"Look."

The area the map pointed them to looked the same as before. Nothing special.

"I don't see it," she said.

He grabbed her by the shoulders and moved her to the right.

"Kneel down a little, let the light catch it."

She did as instructed. The pallor of the grass changed, but nothing stood out.

"Tracks, in the weeds, look."

When he said it, she saw it. A pair of pale stripes in the weeds by the tree line. Tire tracks. They were too faint to see up close. The distance allowed light to reflect off the pale side of grass laid down by a heavy vehicle.

"So he parked the car there."

"And dropped the body."

"Angela," she said.

"Right. He dropped her and he took the car back. It would get him home faster."

"Well, that makes sense, but it gives us two problems."

"No car," he said.

"And no Angela," she said.

Frustrated, she brushed weeds away and walked back to the car.

She wanted to shout, "It never ends!"

Tablet on the hood, she searched the map one more time. Compared it yet again. They were right on top of it. The spot was clear. One thing was certain: within fifteen minutes of their target time, Angela Hoffman had been somewhere in this field, and according to the map, she'd never left.

"I give up," Teri said.

"You know what's funny?" Thomas asked, approaching.

"Nothing?"

"The tracks coming in. One set." He held up a single finger.

She blinked at him. The meaning clear.

"Someone drove in, but no one drove out."

"So how is that possible?"

"I don't know. I'm just stating facts. He came here, he parked over there and then … what?"

She went back to the screen. What were they missing?

Tracing their steps back to the location indicated on the screen, she knelt by the tracks, which were now clear once you knew to look for them. She felt like a special unit detective with none of the training.

"I know what to look for," she said. "I just don't know how to look for it."

"Well, it looks like the car was parked here."

She hit on something.

"For how long?" she said.

He started, came to the same conclusion, she guessed.

"What if he left it?"

"He left it and came back for it later. There's no one out here and he didn't have enough time to dispose of it or her properly. You leave it here, come back when you can do it right."

Thomas rubbed his head again.

"That means it could be anywhere, though."

Following the tracks, she walked the tree line toward a point farther down.

"I don't think so," she said, and went back to the car.

On the hood, she zoomed out of the field. When Thomas came up behind her, she had pulled down the menu.

"Look," she said, and switched the date on the app.

The field of red dots disappeared, all wiped away except for one.

"Son of a bitch."

She nodded through the catch of trees between them and the water.

"She's in the lake."

Ch. 26

Far enough offshore to be submerged, Angela or at least her phone signal had last been verified just past the drop-off within throwing distance of the shore. According to the USGS map Teri pulled up, the max depth at that distance was twenty feet. She checked the next few dates to be certain, but this was where the signal ended. Most phones were water resistant now, so she guessed the battery had died. Standing on the edge of the shore, gazing across the slick black surface, which had grown darker as the sun sank lower, she attempted to discern some sign of the scene below. In the shade of trees, in that depth, all she received was a reflection and a shallow murky haze.

Already picking through the underbrush, Thomas followed close behind.

"All we know for certain is her phone is out there."

"And her car."

"We don't know that."

"It never left—you said that. Do you see anywhere to hide a brand-new Escalade?"

He struggled to answer.

"Besides, look."

At the edge of the trees, where a space wide enough to drive a truck through met the water, deep tire impressions followed a rise in the shore where a heavy vehicle had sunk into the mud.

"Pretty definitive, I'd say."

From the tracks, it was clear someone had run out of road and it looked like they were going fast when they did it. The rise, a few feet higher than the water, looked like a BMX ramp.

"He jumped it?"

She read the tracks, scratching her head. Maybe. It did make sense.

"I guess he did. It's a heavy truck—it would never sink pushing it in. Four-wheel drive, I guess you could get up to speed and clear a few more feet than otherwise."

"No one saw that? Or heard it?"

"There's nothing over here. The power plant and dam on that side, abandoned over here. I bet you can't see this exact spot from anywhere else on the lake."

"OK, how sure are we? If we call someone out and she's not there?"

Teri already had her shoes off, wading into the shallows, which were much colder on this side than at the docks behind the Shores.

"What are you doing?"

"Making sure."

The drop-off was quick. This side had a steeper incline owing to the dam construction on this end of the lake. In seconds she was waist high, fighting through fallen limbs that crisscrossed near the banks, untended for years. At chest level she had to go under to duck beneath and hopefully around the tangle.

"Be right back," she said, and went in.

Jagged edges clawed her as she swam under a gnarled tree limb as thick as she was. The bottom over here was muddy on top of the rocky layer. She sank when her hands touched, going several inches before finding purchase to pull herself through. Once on the other side, she shot up and sucked in a breath of air.

"Where is it?" she called to shore.

Tablet in hand, Thomas directed her to the area where a vehicle should be. A straight line out from the raised edge.

"Looks like right here. I'm standing on the tracks now."

Pointing with his arm, he indicated a spot only a few feet away from her. She swam over, feeling for anything with her feet as they kicked.

"Be right back," she said.

The sun was getting lower and the few inches of visibility underwater was grey, washed out. The car wasn't in the spot from the map, but that didn't mean it wasn't here. GPS was only so accurate and could be off by several feet in any direction. That didn't include water distortion, which she wasn't familiar with. It was also possible only the phone was here, covered over with mud on the bottom, a red herring, but the clues made too much sense. It simply had to be here. Angela had to be out here.

Kicking down, Teri reached the bottom, coated in a thick black slime. Digging through the deposits, she came to the stony bottom and shuffled her hands under the upper layer, searching for a discarded cell phone in a pool of muck. A few minutes in, she came up again, gasping, shaking lake water from her eyes and nose.

"Find anything?"

"Not yet."

"It's not there?"

She didn't want to shout back and forth.

"Hold on."

Under again, this time she went straight to the bottom and positioned herself in the best possible guess of where the SUV should have been. It was big, six feet tall maybe, which meant it was no farther than ten feet down. Facing shore, lined up with where she expected it to be, she pushed back into the lake. The idea was to follow the track off the bank to wherever the beast had come to a stop. The plan ended as fast as it started when she rammed hard into something, a wide edge between her shoulder blades that sent her off to the side. Her hand grasped in the dark and found something cold, hard, metal. The edge was sharp; she couldn't identify it, but it was definitely big.

Feeling with both hands, she found more, a large, flat side panel, plastic, maybe a taillight. The edge she had a hold on curved at a long angle. Like a wheel well. Her fingers found the knobby rubber tread of tires mired in the lake bottom. Moving down the long, smooth body, she made out the contours of a large vehicle, hands sliding across slick glass windows, still intact. Struggling to breathe with excitement, she felt along the roof, found the thin metal strips for the luggage rack, braced on the roof and kicked straight up.

She broke the surface with such force she came half out the water. Thomas jumped onshore, caught off guard. When she came down, caught her breath, slinging mud and silt from her eyes, she threw her arms up, pointing down.

"It's here."

Ch. 27

Teri emerged from the lake. Tendrils of water poured from her skin, hair and clothes. Her shirt clung close and the cool air raised goose bumps across her flesh. She trudged through the muddy shallows to an extended arm, where Thomas helped her the rest of the way. Exhausted, heart thumping and adrenaline shooting through every vein, she fell to the ground, gasped for air and flopped onto her back. Her chest rose and lowered in spastic fits. It was minutes before she could speak.

"She's there. I found it," she said.

Thomas was kneeling, at a loss for words and what to do.

"It's farther out. With the wheels turning, it must have kept going until it got stuck. It's her, it has to be."

"You couldn't see it?"

"Pitch-black. You'd never see anything down there without radar or something."

He looked to where she'd surfaced, farther than they had guessed.

"We can't pull it up with my car. So, now what?"

"Now I dry off."

She got to her feet, wobbly but managing an upright position with help.

"You got any towels?"

"Maybe in the trunk. I don't know."

She held out her hand.

"Keys."

He handed over the fob, fixated on the area of ink black water where the car waited. She trod toward his car, mind buzzing, nerves steeled against the truth.

"Hey, Thomas, I'm real sorry about this."

"About what?" he shouted without turning back as she popped open the driver's side.

"This," she said too low to hear, hopped in and cranked the engine. By the time he realized she was leaving, Teri had backed the car to the road, swung around and started down the long driveway. She saw him, hands in the air, shouting in the red glow of taillights and a cloud of dust. In seconds he was gone.

At the gate, she wished he were there to help her sling its massive weight out of the way. She already knew from experience it was a two-person job. Impulsive and shortsighted—that would be on her gravestone someday.

The nose of the Camry pressed against the bars, she hit the gas until it nudged open. Once on the move, the gate swung in a wide arc and let her pass unobstructed. She was thankful it didn't scrape down the right side of the car this time. When this was over, she'd find a way to buy him a new one, even if he refused to talk to her anymore. Right now, there was something that had to be done, and it was too dangerous to ask someone else to come along.

Pulling into traffic, she had her phone in one hand, dialing with the other as she weaved between lanes. It rang twice before a hushed voice answered.

"What are you doing!"

"Hayley, I need a favor."

When she pulled into the drive and came to a stop at the guardhouse, a tall man in a uniform with a rent-a-cop badge eyed the damage on the door. Perhaps he recognized the car because he made no effort to appear friendly or welcoming as he approached the window. She lowered the glass, a tight-lipped grin the most she could muster.

"Can I help you ... ma'am?"

Hunched over, a step away from the car, he couldn't have said unwelcome louder. If he'd had a gun, his hand would be on it. Any other time she would have taken pleasure in getting him to move, but she was in a hurry. Thomas could get here in fifteen minutes if he ran, and she was sure he would.

"Gardner, I'm a guest."

Matted hair, filthy skin, the suspicion was warranted.

"First name."

"Mine or Hayley's ... Hayley Gardner, 6998 Julian Drive. She called down. You just got off the phone with her. Now please ... move."

Teri rolled up the window for emphasis. This conversation was over.

The man frowned and made a show of strutting back to his outhouse-sized office, but the gate went up and the door to the shack closed, so she drove through. Headlights scanned front lawns, passed over wide porches and thick old-growth trees. Dusk had arrived, making the approach seem even more ominous.

Her hands flexed on the wheel, heart thumping. Around a slow curve, the sloping grounds of Roman's home came into view. She killed the lights, pulled into the drive and stared at the massive home. The lights were on, upstairs and down. In the living room, curtains twitched. Hayley—she was terrified, but not as much as Teri was.

For a moment she sat in the drive, savoring the last few minutes before there was no going back. The black hole where the garage stood open reminded her how bad this could all go. She should park on the street. At least then it would be harder to hide her body. She let herself think. What might happen next, what a terrible idea this really was and how stupid she could be if she really applied herself.

It felt appropriate, watching shadows pass the windows. One, smaller, lingered in the living room. The larger passed through the dining room and disappeared. Otherwise it was quiet. The road behind was still, families already home, tending the responsibilities of modern life. The driveway was silent except for Thomas's engine ticking as it cooled. The curtain twitched again; the shadow moved away.

She pulled the door handle, a spotlight announcing her presence when the overhead came on. *Last chance*. She stepped out, shut the door and stood in darkness. Every bit of concentration it took to move forward, to not stumble on the lighted driveway, to take each step one at a time, hand on the wrought iron railing, served to make her seem more confident. Even if no one could see it, the illusion was important and almost enough to convince herself she wasn't shaking from fear as much as fatigue.

A rigid finger pressed a small white button, followed by the chime of the doorbell. For a moment time stopped; she saw herself being dragged inside, stuffed in the trunk, joining Angela at the bottom of the lake. She saw Thomas, alone in a vacant field. She saw all her mistakes in an instant. Then the door opened.

Ch. 28

Bigger in person, if that was possible, he took up the entire doorway. She had forgotten to account for the foreshortening effects of an overhead view. Now, as he stood in the gap between her and the foyer, illuminated by a golden glow within, she realized how easily he could put this plan to a swift and permanent end.

"Miss Fletcher. Come in." His voice was deep but not intimidating, at least not intentionally.

His massive body took a single step to the side, clearing enough room for her to slip past, a voluntary victim of an apex predator. She ducked as she entered, put as much space between herself and the wall of a man as possible and waited while he shut the door. It latched with a finality that brought a flinch. She felt her balance falter, held strong while Roman gave a long eye down his nose. A heavy hand rested on the door. He studied her, wary. With a sniff he was in charge again.

"This is unexpected."

"You have no idea," she said.

He was a man of intention. His motion for her to enter the dining room a direct gesture with no need for accompanying sentiment. He noticed she was struggling to balance.

"You've come unprepared. Have a seat," he said.

She was unprepared but not in the way he was thinking. Her deepest hope that somehow, she could catch the calculating killer off guard through the least expected approach.

She took a chair nearest the windows at one end of the elegant table. It was dark wood, highly polished with a white runner down the length. Its appearance next to her own made the mud, lake water and stench of algae seem a part of herself. The red and brown smear on her skin a birthmark more than a stain. She also knew this evidence, which he chose to ignore, set the stage between them. The stakes were clear. They both knew what he was. Did she still hold enough secrets?

Hayley was almost eclipsed by her father, cowering behind him as he blocked the doorway to the hall and Teri's only exit. From her seat, the kitchen, with the door to the garage, was too far to reach. She was trapped.

"Upstairs, now." Roman spoke without turning to face his daughter.

The meek girl, eyes wider than should be possible, hung her head as she headed toward the stairs.

"Leave the phone," he said.

With pause, Hayley reached into her pocket, set her phone on a table just inside the dining room and scurried away, but not before shooting Teri a look of concern mixed with a tinge of hope.

"You stay here. I'll be right back."

Teri did as she was told, hands flat on the table. She had no intention of leaving until she got what she wanted or she was dead. That didn't stop her knee from bouncing like a jackhammer as soon as he could no longer see. She made a mental note of everything in the room. She questioned the strength of the windows and their thickness; could they mask a scream? A nervous glance at the camera overhead: its dark eye focused on her and the room beyond.

She strained to make out sound in other rooms as heavy footfalls had ceased somewhere beyond her knowledge and a door shut with a slam. The floorboards once again complained under pressure as they returned. He turned the corner, revealing a scowl that she expected was rarely seen inside the courtroom, where he was so well-known, and a glint at his right hand.

Though dark as night, smooth and half-concealed in his meaty grip, the gun was all she saw as he crossed the room and took a seat opposite. He let himself down into the high-back chair, laid the weapon with a weighted thump between them and brought his hands together in a mock prayer.

"Now, how can I help you?"

Difficult as it was, she forced herself not to look at the object that would be her end. At least it would be quick, painless maybe. Still there was no room for error. Intent on portraying confidence, she looked the monster in the eye and spoke her case.

"I've come to make a deal." Her voice was steady, her jaw locked tight and chin set.

"I don't understand where you feel the leverage is for such a … request, but … I am intrigued to find out."

She studied his face, unsure what he meant.

"Go on," he prompted.

She swallowed hard but continued.

"I know what you did."

"What have I done?" he said. His tone expressed a casual innocence.

"You killed Angela Hoffman. Over there." She nodded to a vacant area of tile.

"And you dumped her body in the lake."

His eyes dropped; they left her face, scanned her chest, arms, landed in her lap. She clenched against his gaze.

"You have a phone on you."

"I do," she said.

"Hand it over."

She resisted the command, reached for her hip, stopped and questioned the wisdom of giving up her best resource in an emergency.

"Now," he stated in a tone that removed doubt.

She slid the device across the table, coming to a stop in front of Roman's right hand. He picked up the gun, raised it overhead and brought the butt down with a crash on the screen. Tiny bits of glass broke free, bounced across the table; a spiderweb erupted on the screen, which went to a prism of color. On the second assault it went dark, dead. Roman brushed the ruined item from the table, replaced the gun and clasped his hands.

"Those are serious accusations and you lack proof ... of any kind."

She'd jumped when the gun came down but recovered, more angry than ever. She lurched forward.

"I saw you and I found the body. You can't run from that. You can work with me or there will be CSI on the scene in five minutes."

"You found a body."

He leaned forward, an eyebrow raised.

"Have you informed the police?"

She went ashen. She could feel the blood drain from her skin before the next sentence came out.

"You should inform a law enforcement official as soon as you discover a crime. Especially one so violent. I would think a young woman of your intelligence would know that." Roman's eyes flicked to the side, focused on something. His jaw clenched.

"I can see you haven't done that. Would you like me to call them for you?"

He was taunting her. *Proceed with the plan.*

A motion in the driveway caught her attention. The shadow that ducked into the open garage moved quick and low. Thomas had arrived faster than expected.

"I was hoping we could discuss matters a little more first."

Roman stood, hand resting on the pistol. The heavy chair screeched as it pushed away.

"I don't see where we have anything to discuss. What you have isn't a deal. It's a request. One I have to decline."

"A plea bargain, then," she shot. His fingers curled.

"You're testing my patience."

"You could kill me but not without raising suspicion. People know I'm involved in this. I could turn you in, but that makes my life a little uncomfortable and you know why."

"Your drug habits are no concern of mine. I'm waiting for you to tell me how this concerns me, and I should tell you, I am not a patient man."

He lifted the gun, tossed it to his left hand, testing the weight.

"You back off and I'll forget this ever happened. We walk away, you have all the evidence. You took everything."

"I have a better plan."

The shot that exploded rang through her ears. The concussion enough to scramble her thoughts, her ears whined an eerie silence beyond its pitch. The shot had not been aimed at her, as she'd expected. Instead wood splintered and burst from the door leading to the garage. Her heart stopped. She was standing, but she didn't remember standing up. The barrel swung around, settled on her chest.

"Sit down."

Braced on trembling arms, she leaned across the table. She was shaking and crying, when did she start crying? A hole no bigger than a finger, the world had screeched to a halt.

"Hey, look at me." He wagged the gun at her.

"Sit down."

She lowered herself to the chair. Head swimming, she could barely listen. Another innocent victim. All of this, to protect Thomas, to take her friend out of the equation, and now …

"You were saying."

She looked up.

"Before we end this little talk, did you have anything else to say?"

"The cameras …" Her words trailed off.

"You're going to need to speak up."

"The cameras … are on," she said. Her eyes traveled to the watchful eye over their heads. A little green light blinked. He followed; the gun stayed put. When he came back, a hatred had taken root.

"We can fix that."

Her leg was rocking now, bouncing out of control. Thoughts racing, the pieces were coming together, but time was running out. Did it even matter now? She had lost; the wager was a failure.

"Good-bye, Miss Fletcher."

Her foot stopped. Her heel planted in the ground and she launched off the chair. On pure impulse, she sprang forward, slammed into the table with her hip, sending a jolt of pain down her side; the redirection sent her careening off course. Stumbling toward Hayley's phone, she tripped, fell and landed hard on her knees. The second explosion ripped through the room. It missed high as she sprawled out, knocked the phone from its perch and rolled. She kicked frantically, crawled around the corner and struggled to gain traction on the wood floor.

She could hear him behind her, huge lumbering steps. A giant coming down the hall. She clutched the phone, no time, hot breath on her heels. Finding her feet, she bounced off the wall, fell to the side and lunged into a bathroom standing open. The door slammed and locked in less time than it took to realize what she was doing.

She spun, stumbled back as heavy fists pounded the wood, or was that her heart? The hinges shook but held. The edge of the tub caught her knees and tumbled her backward into the porcelain hole. Her head hit the wall, elbow banged off the side, stars and violent pain filled her world.

The door shook, wood cracking. She didn't have long. Fumbling with the phone, she found the dialer, tapping out numbers with a shaking hand. A nagging voice asked how long she had, how long before police arrived, would they find Roman, disposing of another body? She corrected the number, twice to get it right, hovered over the call button.

Doorframe snapped, a foot kicking in the door, which was now a gap, soon to be wide open. She swiped through apps looking for a familiar icon, found the right one, opened it and pointed the phone at the door. When the man burst through, the gun was gone, but murderous rage had taken its place.

Teri held out the phone like a talisman, warding off the fate that was coming. Her words tumbled out.

"This is Roman Gardner. He killed Angela Hoffman in his kitchen last Thursday. Now he's trying to kill me."

She turned the phone on herself, a close video of her own frantic features filling the screen. The counter at the top showed thirty-seven viewers on the live broadcast.

"My name is Teri Fletcher. Someone send help, please."

She flipped the phone around, spat the words.

"Live feed, asshole. Make your choice."

Her hands trembled so hard the video would be nothing but a blur, but she kept the camera pointed at him. Where there had been rage, a kind of blind hate flooded. The back side of a meaty hand slapped the phone away. She yelped. He grabbed her foot, yanked her leg, which jerked her down into the tub, smacked her head again on the edge and left her at his mercy. When he came over the lip, she kicked, caught him in the jaw. The next time he grabbed her legs, crushed them against her chest. Fingers clawed at her throat, reaching for the jugular. She twisted and screamed, braced her arms on the tile, fought with all her might. It was no use. She was overpowered; it was all over but the concession. A fist landed in her ribs, something snapped and she howled, kicked hard again and managed to land one in the center of his chest.

Off guard, Roman stumbled back, fell into the hall, caught himself on the doorframe. An alarm went off. Ear-piercing sirens filled the house, rocketed down the hallway. He turned, an animal expression on his face. The third shot rang out. Time stood still. The rage fell, and Roman's face dropped to a scowl of etched features. A lifetime of disgust distilled into a single expression. Marred only by the red trickle escaping his mouth, then nose. He fell like a redwood, hard enough to shake the house, dropping just out of view. His legs the only thing Teri could see following the crash. A second thunk, down the hall, followed by sobbing.

Sirens somewhere in the distance. Teri fell back into the tub, ready to accept whatever happened next.

Ch. 29

Teri's fingers traveled the keys in swift strokes. Familiar patterns they had traced a thousand times or more. In minutes a live feed from a courthouse downtown appeared, the banner across the bottom from one of the many local stations covering today's hearing. As loud as she could without disturbing anyone, she turned up the volume to hear the report as it came in.

... for his part in the corruption scandal. Officer Mark Wallace has received a sentence of twenty-five years including counts of obstruction, extortion, theft and attempted murder. The former Buncombe County sheriff has yet to be tried on a separate count of accessory to murder in the case of Assistant City Attorney, Angela Hoffman. If convicted, Wallace could see an extended sentence including life behind bars. The local attorney's office ...

She lowered the volume, heard stirring in the other room. A few moments later Thomas walked out, scratching his head, a deep yawn escaping into the late morning air. A grey and white tabby darted between his feet.

He looked better. The stress of the court cases, the endless rounds of questioning and his recovery from the gunshot—which, thank God, had missed anything vital—had taken its toll on them both. Now, months removed from the worst of it, he looked stronger, more rested, eyes no longer sunken and hollow.

"They should just shoot him," he said, and headed to the kitchen. He poured a cup of kibble into a silver dish on the floor.

"Didn't mean to wake you," she said.

"Not a problem. I'm missing the good stuff."

He went straight for the coffeemaker, which had prepared a fresh cup at the usual time, about two hours after she got up.

"I love this timer. Don't know why I never used mine."

One of the few things that survived the disaster in her old place, the coffeepot sat in a place of honor on the kitchen counter, a memorial to the power of endurance. Aside from the cherished coffeemaker, a few boxes with odds and ends also resided in what had been Thomas's place downtown.

Now shared between them, it offered a view of the park, where joggers ran in the morning, and dog walkers chased after their charges with plastic bags, and even a glimpse of the Swannanoa just beyond that: a major upgrade from the busy downtown streets she had overlooked before. It also smelled better, most of the time. She had even received a private space, where Thomas had set up a desk for her in the corner by a window. It was too good to be true. But as with most things these days, she was learning to appreciate what she had in front of her and try not to question too much.

It was peaceful and quiet. She had the place to herself in the daytime when he was at work, and they spent their evenings together, usually in, watching movies and chowing down on microwave burritos. Sometimes she even cooked, but that was a rare and delicate ordeal, better left to those more talented in the kitchen. They were happy and the arrangement worked. On the rare occasion she brought up finding a new place, he dismissed the subject with a casual wave.

"No rush, whenever you're ready." She wasn't in a rush.

"It's too bad we won't get to see Roman's face when they haul him off to prison."

"No one is ever seeing that monster's face again," she said. "Except in the obituaries, and that's fine by me. He got everything he deserved."

After a life spent intimidating others, she found it poetic that he hadn't learned to recognize the capacities of his own child. A hard man and ruthless, he'd ruled with an iron fist, possibly most harshly at home, where the budding flower he sought to overshadow had learned too much from her father and his brand of justice. When Hayley found the gun Roman left on the table, the one he'd set aside to take care of Teri the way he had Angela, she didn't think twice to use it. She told Teri during the hearings that she had intended only to set off the alarms, to call the police so he would stop. She hadn't even known Thomas was lying in the garage, bleeding out from a chest wound. She saw the gun, knew no help would arrive in time and made the choice. There was no thought to it. Only a decision that had to be made and no time to think about the consequences. Teri wanted to ask her if she'd do it again, but the answer was unspoken between them. They were glad he was gone.

Teri and Hayley were both cleared of charges when they agreed to work with the prosecutor to expose the cops like Officer Wallace who were working outside the system. With the information Teri and Thomas had gathered and the location of Angela Hoffman's body, the city was able to uncover the depths of Roman's crooked deals and take down a series of high-ranking city officials with knowledge of the crimes.

Thomas received probation for obstructing an investigation and was released, since his lawyer argued that he had attempted to report the crime on the night he was locked up and that circumstances within the department made it impossible for him to feel safe doing so again. Teri and Hayley agreed to work with the prosecutor. At trial, they came across as victims, and heroines, who had been coerced and bullied into keeping their secret until the night Teri confronted Roman at his home. The news outlets went nuts with the story; it was months before they lost interest, and even now it was hard to go out in public without feeling the eyes of a small town who knew there was a local celebrity in their midst, one known for her actions against one of the town's elite.

In the end, the DA looked the other way on the trafficking charges, since the evidence had been destroyed by a police-issue sidearm. He took Teri's and Hayley's testimony on the murder, and with the tape of Roman cleaning the scene, the body and the lack of a defendant, he called it an open-and-shut case. The corruption probe lagged on and on, stretching into infinite bureaucratic red tape, traveling down long dark alleys into back rooms. A process that might never truly end.

Thomas sat on the edge of the desk, mug in hand. He really looked a lot better now, and Teri thanked whoever watched over her for sending one of their own to keep her safe. He sipped his coffee, studying her in the bright light of her little corner. Another change for the better.

"Gonna stay inside and watch videos all day?"

She peeked through the blinds. No one outside, no crews in vans waiting for a reaction. They were old news. Roman was dead, Wallace was going away, maybe for life, and she had made Hayley promise to keep in touch, to call if she needed anything, anything at all. The girl had said she would.

Teri closed the lid and got to her feet.

"Not today."

Acknowledgments

No man is an island and no worthwhile project is accomplished without the support of many others behind the scenes. I would like to offer my heartfelt thanks and deepest gratitude for the following (non-exhaustive list of) people who have helped me along the way.

First and foremost to Anna Ray who has dealt with my years long quest to become a published author and many shoebox novels I ended up with in the process. Your support is priceless and truly the only reason I succeed. Also many thanks to a close friend and critiquing partner Roger Gorex, who always has a new idea and new reason to get excited about doing the work. To my brother Christopher who has seen me try so many things and succeed now and then. Douglas Bramlett who endured countless questions on obscure subject matter, Trey Tallon and Brian Stanley for their assistance with procedurals, all the wonderful beta readers who took the time to guide this work to completion: Eve Hoffman, Krystle Rose and Hollie Hausenfluck for assistance in early revisions. My editor, Michele Alpern, William Aicher & the Indie Author's Coalition and Sarah VanDeBogert. Special thanks to Johnny and Regina Ray who have treated me like one of their own from day one.

A note of gratitude to friends and family who have been supportive. Including but not limited to: My parents Sara and Joey, who encouraged creativity in all its forms and my daughter, Isabelle who has inspired me to be a better person. John Questore, Benjamin K. Bachman, Scott Brown, Nova Jamerson, the Twitter writer community and many many more

About the Author

Jason Stokes is an author and artist living in the mountains of western North Carolina. When he's not at work in the studio he's raising a pair of indomitable Cornish Rex cats and travelling the world with his wife and best friend, Anna.

Don't Miss

Ghost Story

October 2019